The Trouble-free Dog

The
Trouble-free
Dog

ROBERT ALLEYNE

Illustrated by Cécile Curtis

ROBERT HALE · LONDON

© Robert Alleyne 1999
Illustrations © Cécile Curtis 1999
First published in Great Britain 1999

ISBN 0 7090 6494 2

Robert Hale Limited
Clerkenwell House
Clerkenwell Green
London EC1R 0HT

2 4 6 8 10 9 7 5 3 1

Typeset in North Wales by
Derek Doyle & Associates, Mold, Flintshire.
Printed in Great Britain by
St Edmundsbury Press Ltd, Bury St Edmunds
and bound by
WBC Book Manufacturers Limited, Bridgend

To Fiona and Connor, who have been my inspiration, and to Cécile Curtis, who was the driving force behind the initial concept of this book.

Contents

Foreword by John Rogerson   10
Introduction: The Development of the Domestic Dog   13

Part I: How to Have a Trouble-free Dog   **17**

1   Choosing the Right Dog for You   19
2   Dogs and Children   40
3   How Many Dogs Are Too Many Dogs?   52
4   A Member of the Family?   61
5   Good Health   67
6   To Neuter or Not to Neuter   79
7   Identification   87
8   Communication (What I Tell Him – What He Hears)   90
9   Crime and Punishment   96
10 Obedience Training: The Modern Approach   102
11 Dogs and the Law   125

Part II: Re-educating the Troubled Dog   **133**

12 The Behavioural Interview   135
13 Aggression   138
14 Excessive Attention-seeking   179
15 Separation Anxieties (Dogs That Can't Bear
      Being Alone)   187
16 Excessive/Inappropriate Barking   201
17 Dogs That Are Sensitive to Certain Sounds   209

Useful Addresses   214
Recommended Reading   216
Index   219

Foreword

I cannot recall how many years have passed by since my very first meeting with Robert Alleyne but I can remember getting that feeling that this was a guy who seemed to have a real sense of feeling for the animals that more and more were beginning to be a part of his life. I got to know Robert much better when he attended some of my week-long residential courses where students spend most of the day listening to lectures, part of the day training dogs and where evenings are for relaxing and swapping tall dog stories. Robert proved to be one of those students who had managed to excel at staying awake and alert during even the most boring of my lectures and also distinguished himself each evening by telling taller dog stories than anyone else present, and all with a great sense of humour. As for the dog training, it is customary for students to be given a dog to work with for the week, the plan being to attempt to train the dog to carry out one of many complex tasks that I was in the habit of dreaming up in order to frustrate the students. The purpose behind this of course, is, to enhance their human–canine communication skills. Robert found himself with two of my most frustrating dogs as he clearly already possessed good basic training skills. These dogs had already left better trainers with their credibility in tatters, not you understand because they were aggressive but simply because they appeared to have an exceptional talent for doing almost exactly the opposite of what the trainer was trying to teach them. At the end of a long afternoon training dogs, Robert was always the one who managed to smile while others often looked decidedly dejected after a typical score of dogs 10 – trainers 0! What became apparent during these revealing courses was the fact that Robert was not only achieving something with the dogs he was given but he actually seemed to be enjoying the challenge.

To be successful as a dog trainer/behaviourist a person requires several different skills, bearing in mind that it is not just the dogs that need help for it is often the owners who have inadvertently caused problems for their pets due to a basic lack of understanding. So in order to provide a useful service one needs to be good at the practical skill of training dogs, to be conversant with the theory of applied canine behaviour and to have great personal communication skills with people. A great sense of humour also helps more than you could ever imagine! Robert possesses all of these skills in abundance and represents all that is good about the modern way of dealing with training and behaviour problems in pet dogs.

Robert's career as an animal warden presents him with daily opportunities to practice and hone the canine and human communication skills that form such a vital part of his work, and few have managed to have more of an impact on a community in an inner city than Robert. His creativity, willingness to learn and love of animals makes Robert ideally suited to the career that he has chosen for himself.

Now I have to be honest and say I have never felt it to be of any great benefit for a dog owner to read books that have been written about dog training or, even less, to read books on dog behaviour as most books tend to oversimplify the intricacies of the relationship between the dog and its owner. No book has ever been published that will answer even the most basic of questions because they are all written from too much of a human viewpoint. Having read through some sample pages of this book I am tempted to change my opinions for what you will read is probably fairly close to how a dog would have written it! And I do mean that in the most complimentary way possible.

All of the characters in this book are real, all of the stories are true, all of the sentiments expressed are genuine and maybe, just maybe, by reading this book, owners will be better able to understand and communicate with their dogs.

John Rogers

Introduction:
The Development of the
Domestic Dog

Of all our fellow creatures, it is only with dogs that man has developed a true mutual allegiance. This very special symbiotic relationship has existed for as long as 14,000 years. Indeed, current research suggests that men first shared the warmth of their fires, the shelter of their caves and the bounty of their hunting with a sort of semi-domesticated wolf, 140,000 years ago. This was not a one-way street however, as these early canines gave them back warmth and guarded their dwelling places in return, as well as having the ability and endurance to outrun and then encircle the prey that their human comrades hunted.

As a pack animal, the wolf is undoubtedly one of the most efficient of all predators, possessing a high degree of intelligence and the ability to co-operate with the other members of his pack to hunt in organized groups. Most of the methods employed in dog training rely very much on this sense of co-operation. The concept that the wolf is the dog's direct ancestor may seem alien, until one compares them with many of the present dog breeds, such as the Alaskan Malamute, the Husky or the Samoyed, who are facially almost identical. There are other possible predecessors, such as the jackal, particularly the longer-legged varieties such as the golden *Canis aureus* or *Canis simensis*, whose outward resemblance to a German Shepherd Dog is quite striking, except that they are little more than half its size. In contrast however, *Canis lupus*, the Grey or Timber Wolf, can be both larger and heavier than even the tallest of our domestic breeds – the Irish Wolfhound and the Great Dane. Dogs are pack animals, as is the wolf, whereas the jackal is primarily a solitary creature, living and hunting alone or in pairs. Wolves often have pale eye colouring, blue or yellow-green, according to the lightness of their fur. Old English Sheepdogs, merle Border Collies and Weimaraners, all exhibit this additional throwback to the lupines.

The great diversity of existing breeds is partly due to the variation amongst early canines, differing according to their places of origin. The present, widely differing forms (so the theory goes) are 'watered down' versions of these multifarious ancestors. Another contributing factor is man's selective breeding of dogs to fulfil different needs such as herding, hunting and guarding, or merely to serve as small, puppy-like lapdogs.

The dogs' role in human activities became ever more sophisticated, as they were trained to herd livestock, pull carts, entertain audiences by wearing clothes and doing comical (if somewhat degrading) tricks, plus take on the grimmer task of participating in actual warfare. Through recent, remarkably advanced methods of training and expansion of dogs' intelligence, they have attained a more elevated status. They have become the eyes, ears, hands or feet of people who are disabled, as well as acting as lifeguards, performing dramatic rescues from drowning, and locating victims lost in snow or earthquakes. It is certainly now accepted by the medical profession that dogs can also help to cure man's physical or psychological ailments, as well as helping us to live a longer, happier and more active life.

When dogs are used for dangerous and complicated tasks, such as detecting drugs, locating explosives, or tracking down and confronting armed criminals, their handlers make something of a game out of the exercise. They take advantage of the canine's ever-present desire for play, channelling it into this exacting work. Of all the ways in which we benefit from them, the most prevalent and obvious is the constant comfort and companionship enjoyed by millions of dog owners. We share with them that unique ability to take pleasure in playful, juvenile activities, throughout our lives. It is this 'Peter Pan' quality which most attracts us and engenders a parental attitude towards them, notwithstanding their age or size.

Pet behaviour counselling only began to emerge into public awareness in the late eighties. Before that, practitioners of this new science were often jokingly described as 'pet shrinks', and were not taken very seriously. Today, they are increasingly being recognized as the saviours of both pet owners and the animals themselves, usually described as 'man's best friend'. The dog, regardless of its size or appearance, is now generally considered to be a direct descendant of the wolf, and this has had a universal influence on the understanding of its mentality, training and treatment.

Dog behaviourists can reconcile distraught owners, seemingly unable to cope with their 'problem pets', who would otherwise be forced to make the heart-breaking decision of taking the animal to a rescue centre. There it would become just another among thousands of homeless creatures who sadly are often referred to as 'second-hand dogs' (or, if they are really unlucky, third, fourth or fifth).

Cécile Curtis

Part I

How to Have a
Trouble-free Dog

1 Choosing the Right Dog for You

One of the reasons that there is such a call for behaviourists and dog trainers is that too many people don't give enough thought to the dog that they choose. All too often, they let their hearts rule their heads. They choose the dog that looks the cutest, or the one that is the first to approach them when they look at the litter. Perhaps they go for the fluffiest, most teddy-bear-like, or the one that growls and seems like it will be a good guard dog. There are those who will choose the puppy that sits right at the back, and is afraid to come forward, as they worry that no one else will pick him.

Potentially, all of these dogs could end up being major problems for their owners if they do not recognize that in spite of all of the things that may have drawn them to that particular puppy, he is still a dog. He will grow up as clever and able to manipulate his environment and the people in it as any other dog, and in some cases more so.

If you're looking for a puppy

The first thing you should do once you have decided that you want a dog is to ascertain who in the family is going to be responsible for which tasks. Who will be the one to walk it? Who will feed it? Who is going to clean up after it? This can often throw up arguments that are best dealt with *before* the dog arrives home. This way, at least in principle, everyone knows where they stand right from the start. If there are small children involved, do not rely on them to keep their promises to clean up after it, or to do anything else they absolutely swear they will. Generally, all young children want is a puppy that is cute and accessible whenever they feel inclined to it, the same as the rest of their toys. To get them to commit to being responsible for maintaining it is probably asking a little too much.

Having decided who is going to do what, you need to discuss what type of dog you want *as a family*. What size dog are you going to be looking for? Will it have long or short hair? Will it be a pedigree or a crossbreed? Make a list of criteria for your ideal dog. If one of you wants a big dog and the rest want a small one, it would probably be best either to go with the majority, or to compromise and pick a medium-sized dog that everyone will be happy with.

The next step is to go to a library that has a variety of books on dogs, or else buy a good book with details on as many breeds of dog as possible. When choosing a book, look for one that goes into the disadvantages of each breed as well as the advantages. Some books simply copy the standard for the breed that is stated by the Kennel Club, which tends to focus on each breed's virtues, without paying too much attention to its faults. Having picked your book, short-list breeds that fit your criteria, in terms of size, coat, typical temperament and so on.

You will probably have to whittle these dogs down still further. Try asking several different dog trainers, vets and behaviourists for their opinions on the breeds you have selected. They will have seen them at their best and worst, and may be able to prepare you for any problems before you choose that type of dog.

You should now have got down to one or two breeds. Having done so, you can contact the Kennel Club (their details are under *Useful Addresses*). They can furnish you with a list of breeders, or, if you want to rescue a dog, a list of rescue centres for the breeds you have chosen.

When actually choosing your puppy, take a little time to study the litter to ensure that you pick the puppy that is most likely to suit you and your lifestyle. This is a point that is very often overlooked, but it can mean the difference between your dog growing old with you, or being put up for rehoming. Take some time to observe the puppies each time that you visit them, and try to go and see them several times before you choose one.

Many people fall for the puppy that is consistently the first to approach them when they go to look at them. But what will this puppy be like when it grows up? Well, firstly, he has shown a complete lack of fear of strangers, so may well be the sort who will run up to everyone he meets with equal enthusiasm as he gets older, which may not always be appropriate. He has also demonstrated that he has no hesitation in deserting his pack to explore something that has taken his interest, which may be a problem when he goes to live with his 'human pack'. He may well be the most dominant puppy in the litter, having spent his life competing successfully against all comers, and may carry on this behaviour when you get him home, where he only has you and your family to practise on. This can lead to a dog that is a bully, both to the family that he lives with, and towards other dogs, which could obviously make both him and you rather unpopular in the local park. On the other hand, he may be the ideal puppy for a family with very boisterous, slightly older children, as he will not grow up frightened of them – though he will need controlling so that he does not end up intimidating them instead. He would also be suitable for someone who wants to spend plenty of time on training him, so he should not necessarily be discounted.

What about the opposite puppy, the one who sits at the back and lets all the others go to greet the new people while he refuses to move? Is he a better bet? Actually, he may be even more of a problem than the previous one. He is exhibiting a fear of strangers and new stimuli, and if he is that nervous at three to six weeks, he could be considerably worse when he is older, unless he is brought out of it as he grows. Although he can be taught to like strangers, it will require some considerable work on the part of the owner. So if you choose this puppy, seek advice from a behaviourist as soon as possible, preferably even before you bring him home. Although he may not be the right choice for someone who lives alone, and wants a confident, outgoing dog, but has few visitors to help familiarize him with new people and get him over his fear he may be ideal for a family with older children. They may well be prepared to take the time to socialize him correctly, without putting him under too much pressure.

What about the puppy in the middle? It doesn't necessarily charge straight up to every new thing that it encounters, having the sense to wait until it is sure that it is safe to do so, usually after waiting to see what happens to that first fearless pup, and maybe even a couple of the others. This puppy will probably be the most responsive to training, and, if taught correctly, should be fairly reliant on it's owner without being too clingy – ideal! Whichever one you choose, it will need some form of training. Even if you fall for the wrong puppy for you, you can still make a success of it, if you get some early advice about how to turn it into the right puppy.

You may decide to get your pup from a pet shop. This may not be such a good idea. Most reputable breeders like to know where their puppies are and who owns them. A pedigree dog that has registration papers carries the reputation of the breeder, which can generally be trusted. Most decent breeders will not sell their puppies to pet shops as they would then be unable to keep tabs on them, preferring instead to sell directly to the customer. So where do pet shops get their puppies from? Well, a few come from the accidental mating of dogs from private owners. However, the vast majority of pet shops get their puppies either directly from puppy farmers, or from local agents who buy farmed puppies, then sell them to the shops themselves for a profit. For the pet shop, this is a way of buying pedigree puppies relatively cheaply, and selling them for a considerable profit, often making over one hundred per cent per puppy. Many of these pups will have come from farms in and around Wales and Ireland, and may have been travelling for hundreds of miles prior to being sold. The farm conditions are often terrible, and many puppies either die on the farm, or on the journey to the shop or agent. Those that survive frequently arrive with forged papers; some may even be crossbreeds that are being sold as pedigrees. So it can be very risky to get a puppy in this way.

Now you need to consider the expense involved in maintaining the dog you have chosen. On top of the purchase price, there will be many other less obvious expenses that you will need to think about. There will be the cost of vaccination, for example. This will vary from one surgery to another, so this will be a good opportunity to find your local vets and introduce yourself. Some of them will have 'starter packs', full of advice on getting and rearing a puppy, that they give to prospective owners. You can also discuss the cost of things like worming, neutering and insurance. Your puppy will need worming several times before it reaches adulthood. Then, as an adult, it will need to be wormed at least every six months to be sure of keeping it worm-free. If you are going to neuter your dog when it is older, it might be a good idea to start saving before you even get the puppy. Neutering is quite an expensive operation, and you don't want an accidental mating to occur just because, when the time came, you couldn't afford the cost of neutering the dog. Insurance can be a huge benefit if your dog should become seriously ill and need an operation or long-term drug therapy. These bills can run into thousands of pounds.

Some breeds, such as Poodles, West Highland White Terriers and Schnauzers, do not moult, and lose very little hair naturally, and so need to be either stripped or clipped to keep their coats in good condition. Stripping involves literally pulling out hair that has grown too long. There are special combs and knives available to assist in performing this task but it should not be attempted unless under the supervision of someone experienced. Clipping basically involves the use of a set of electric clippers to trim or cut the fur to a desired length, rather like shearing a sheep. You can either send the dog off to the grooming parlour every couple of weeks, or you can learn to do this yourself. Although this will save you the cost of paying someone else to do it, you will obviously have to pay for the necessary equipment, and the time involved in doing it.

If you're looking for an older dog

Think very carefully about the type of dog you are looking for *before* you actually go looking for it, and be determined to get the type of dog you had planned. Don't settle for something that wasn't what you were looking for: you may regret it later and wish that you had held out for the one that you wanted.

Choosing an older dog is much the same as choosing a puppy, and you should take the time to read the previous section before reading this one. However, there is one very important difference when opting for an adult dog. Although some dogs will be up for re-housing due to marriage break-ups, the death of an owner, or for health reasons such as a family member with an allergy, most older dogs are being rehomed because they are already causing some problem or other for their current owners. It is therefore quite possible that you may inherit that problem when you take on the dog.

It may have already learned to dislike particular things. Perhaps the original owners had children who were rough with it, and now it is frightened of children. Or maybe they allowed it to chase small animals such as cats and squirrels, and it now had a predatory aggression. Or perhaps it was under-socialized and is now nervous of strangers. It could be that it is destructive when left, or is still not house-trained. It may have learnt to be aggressive towards other dogs. It pays to try to find a dog with a known history, so that you can be as sure as possible that the dog will fit in with you and your family. Having said that, you shouldn't necessarily reject a dog simply because nothing is known about its previous owners. Most rescue centres will spend some considerable time assessing a dog's character while it is in their care, so will be able to offer some advice on that score.

There are definite advantages to choosing an older dog. You know exactly what the dog is going to look like. You know how big it will be, whether its coat will be long or short, and what it's temperament is like. It may well come house-trained, and have already gone through its destructive puppy phase. It may also come partially or even fully obedience trained, saving you having to teach the dog to perform basic exercises.

The thing to bear in mind is that whichever you choose, you are going to have some work to do. Adult or puppy, it is still going to have to learn where it fits in your household and what the rules are.

Inherited characteristics

When acquiring a dog, owners often make a very serious oversight that frequently ends up costing both them and their dog dearly. They don't stop and take into consideration the type of dog they are considering getting, and what function that breed was intended to perform.

Working dogs

For example, many owners who take on **Border Collies** find that the dogs develop behavioural problems. The sheer intelligence of the breed means that they need a great deal of mental stimulation. Often, however, they are taken on by people who fail to provide this – perhaps young parents living in a small, high-rise flat who are kept busy with the children, or elderly people who may not be able to give the dog the vast amount of exercise it requires. This breed was developed to herd sheep, and to spend several hours doing it. They have been selectively bred for a great many years for stamina and endurance – to work outdoors, and shrug off the cold and wet. Above all though, they were designed to use their consider-able intellect. This is not a breed that will lie by the fire all day not wanting to do much of anything. When confined in a domestic environment, they have a leaning towards particular types of problems. Destruction seems to be a particularly common problem with collies that are left alone for long peri-ods. Noise is also often a problem, with neighbours complain-ing about them howling and barking when left. Predatory and chase behaviours are very common in collies as well, as this behaviour was encouraged when they were being bred as sheepdogs. Many collies chase bicycles or joggers. Some chase vehicles, snapping at the tyres as though they were sheep that needed moving on. These will often be dogs that have no experience of farm work.

Case History – Red is for danger

One collie owner I visited had a dog that had a particular dislike of red cars. At the sight of one he would throw himself at it, roaring ferociously, desperately trying to break free from the owner so that he could tear it wheel from wheel. What caused this extension of the innate predatory behaviour remains unclear. The dog had never been in a red car, not had it ever been run over or even nearly run over. To the best of the owner's knowledge, the dog had never even been startled by a red car, although it is possible that the owner missed something that upset the dog.

To cure the dog, we had to teach him a different attitude towards cars, red ones in particular. To do this, I use the same method as for fear-based aggression, rewarding the dog with treats or toys whenever it is exposed to the stressful stimulus (see under *Aggression*). However, it is often not enough to reward the dog, as some dogs will consider chasing a car to be far more rewarding than a piece of food or a favourite toy. I added a consequence to ignoring a 'LEAVE' or 'NO' command, so that the owner could use that if the dog should ignore the reward. I recommended they use a can with pebbles in it (sound deterrents are discussed on p.177).

The **Rough Collie** (Lassie Collie) is a rather more sensitive breed, and can be a little nervous. They are often wary of children. However, they are a working breed, and can develop a very close relationship with their owners.

The **Boxer** by comparison is a natural performer, and loves to play to an audience. They are extremely powerful, with a deep chest and a compact body built for speed and endurance. Indeed they never seem to tire. They can be very stubborn in temperament, particularly males, who can be aggressive towards other males, but they have few, if any, common behavioural problems. They are generally very good with people, particularly children.

In **German Shepherds** you see several behaviour characteristics that relate to the type of work the breed was meant to do. As a guarding breed, they almost invariably have a fierce loyalty to their owners and often to one owner in particular. As a dog bred to guard and work sheep, they tend to want to keep their human flock together, and will usually become stressed if members of the family do not stay together when out on a walk. They also tend to have problems with things like territorial aggression and fear-based aggression, the former because they are a guarding breed, and the latter due to a combination of being bred for guarding, coupled with breeders using dogs with nervous temperaments. Bred to work closely with an owner/handler, they are generally very responsive to training, and are perhaps the most versatile working breed. They are used for guarding, guiding, herding, search and rescue, and assistance work for the disabled. The police and the military in this and many other countries also use them for drug work, tracking, finding arms and bombing equipment, and for apprehending criminals on the run.

However, they are very prone to a medical condition called hip dysplasia. In this, the hip joints become damaged through daily exercise, which causes pressure on the ball and socket joint in the hip. Exercise causes tiny cracks to appear in the bone itself, and new bone forms over the cracks causing uneven ridges. These points become vulnerable to arthritis as the dog gets older. Other breeds can also get this condition, though it is primarily associated with German Shepherds.

There are other breeds that, while they may have been bred to serve similar purposes, have developed very different temperament characteristics. The **Dobermann Pinscher**, for example, was bred as a guard dog, intended to protect its owner and his property from any threat. The Dobermann is a breed known to act on its own initiative, and when provoked will often bite anyone it feels inclined to. It also tends to give very little warning. This may be because Dobermanns are generally less fearful than some other breeds such as the German Shepherd, so have less reservations about a confrontation. Certainly the services have been reluctant to use them because of the difficulty in controlling them in an aggressive situation.

As a behaviourist, I see very few Dobermanns with fear-based aggression problems. Dominant aggression is, however, far more common than in many other breeds. They are also prone to behaviours such as flank-sucking and lick lesions, caused by the dog repeatedly licking at a particular spot, usually on a leg or foot. This is usually a stress-related behaviour and often occurs in dogs in rescue centres and boarding kennels.

The **Old English Sheepdog** is one of the best known of our breeds, and has universal appeal. It is very much a working animal and was designed to herd sheep and move cattle. They can be wary of strangers, and make very vocal guard dogs. Recently, they seem to have become a little nervous in temperament.

The much maligned **Rottweiler** has acquired a reputation that may be somewhat unjustified. Although it is unquestionably a fierce guard dog, capable of inflicting serious injury on whoever or whatever has made the mistake of annoying it, it rarely seems to do so. Certainly, breeders have worked very hard to encourage the good-natured side of the dog, which was as a drover and guard, and has mastiff and sheepdog origins. At the time of writing this book, I have never been called to deal with a Rottweiler with behavioural problems, despite the fact that they are still popular, certainly more popular than some of the breeds that I have already mentioned. That is not to say that they do not have any problems, certainly they do. It just seems that the owners either know how to deal with them, or are not bothered with putting them right. Generally very good with people, particularly children, Rottweilers are nonetheless fearsome guards, and an intruder enters their territory at his peril. Males in particular tend to be very dominant, and often dislike other male dogs, especially other male Rottweilers.

Gundogs

Of the gundog breeds, the **Golden Retriever** has for many years been known as a gentle giant, friendly and affectionate to all it meets. Most owners would tell you that if someone broke into their house, their goldie would drown him in a sea of slobber. This has meant that they have been known until very recently as very good 'family dogs'. But in the last few years their temperaments seem to have become somewhat less amenable. I am seeing more aggression problems in this breed than I ever have, and I know of colleagues and breeders who have said the same. Food aggression is on the increase in Golden Retrievers, and more so in the gundog group in general than in any other. I am also seeing more dominant aggression in goldies than I have previously. It may be down to breeding from too many dogs with aggressive tendencies.

Nonetheless, despite the picture I have portrayed, the Golden Retriever is still on the whole a loving, friendly dog. If you are careful about where you buy your puppy from, and rear it correctly, there is no reason why yours should not be too.

Closely related to the Golden Retriever is the **Labrador Retriever**. Its versatility is remarkable. Used as a guide dog, police dog, and search and rescue dog, it is also used as a sniffer dog, finding drugs, bombs and other weapons. All this from a dog that was originally bred to retrieve game. It was developed from the **Newfoundland**, a huge, dense-coated water dog, whose job was to pull in fishermen's nets.

They generally have sound temperaments, particularly bitches. Males have a tendency to be ruled by their sex drive, and so often have sex-related problems. Labradors are also renowned gannets, and will usually eat almost anything. For a short-coated breed, they tend to moult rather heavily.

Some of the spaniels also have very specific behaviours inherent within their breeds. 'Rage syndrome', a type of aggression for no obvious reason, has become a very real, though uncommon problem. A dog with this condition could one minute be lying in front of the fire, and the next be hanging off its owners arm, trying to tear her limb from limb. It appears to be most common in the **Cocker Spaniel**, and particularly in dogs that are all one colour, most notably 'red' ones. Food obsession is again a problem with spaniels, and logically, so is food aggression.

A good **Irish Setter** is a magnificent-looking animal. When well-groomed, the gorgeous, deep red coat is quite stunning. On the other hand, it is not a breed known for its intelligence, and can be difficult to train. They are not in any way fussy about what they eat. In fact, as long as it is edible, a setter will usually consume it with relish.

The **Weimaraner** is another striking breed. The coat is a unique shade of grey, and it usually has pale eyes, either bluish grey or amber in colour. It has a very strong character, and the males in particular are known to have a dominant streak. It is not uncommon for them to try to take over the entire household. The males are also often aggressive towards other dogs, especially other males.

Toy dogs

The **Cavalier King Charles Spaniel**, on the other hand, is renowned for its excellent temperament. I have only ever met one aggressive one, and that was more the fault of the owner than the dog. However, they are prone to eye and ear problems.

Terriers

The terrier group are possibly the most misunderstood group of dogs when it comes to the average potential new dog owner. Because most of the terrier breeds are quite small, people forget that they were designed to do a job of work. That work usually involved using a high level of aggression on some unsuspecting victim. Although a popular pet dog, the **Jack Russell** was bred to hunt and kill small animals, and often shows high aggression towards other animals, including other dogs. They are very vocal, and people often choose them as burglar deterrents, as they are quick to bark. The same is true of **West Highland White Terriers**, **Scottish Terriers** and **Cairn Terriers**. The owners are often dismayed by the violent reaction of many of these breeds when confronted by something they do not like. The aggression that has for many years been a desirable trait in these breeds often becomes their undoing as a pet dog.

Designed to be super-confident, terriers often take over the entire household, although the owners mistakenly think that a small dog would be much easier to control and train. Many of these dogs were bred to be independent and act on their own initiative. Subsequently, if they are not correctly trained and influenced when they are very young, they have a tendency to show very dominant behaviours. Fouling indoors, taking possession of areas of the house such as beds or chairs and stealing can all be manifestations of dominance, as well as aggression towards people or other dogs.

The **Staffordshire Bull Terrier** is a much underrated little dog. Yes, it was bred as a fighting dog, baiting bulls and bears, and it can certainly be aggressive towards other dogs. But the responsible breeders of these dogs have worked very hard to improve the temperaments of the breed, and their efforts have paid dividends. It is wise to remember that they may still enjoy the odd scrap or two, especially with dogs of the same sex. In general, though, they are extremely friendly with people, particularly children, as they are real clowns and enjoy being silly. If you are considering this breed, it would be an error to overlook it because of media hype.

The **English Bull Terrier** was developed for a similar purpose to the Staffordshire, but has a somewhat less reliable temperament. They are very powerful, and are known to be stubborn and difficult to train. They can be unpredictable, and can go from being placid to aggressive with no warning whatsoever. Males in particular have a tendency towards dominant aggression, often towards their owners, so anyone thinking of obtaining one should seek advice on ensuring that it never becomes a problem.

The Spitz breeds such as **Huskies**, **Chow Chows** (actually classified as a utility dog), **Samoyeds** and **Malamutes** are perhaps the nearest to their wolf ancestors, and have maintained many characteristics from that wild lineage. They are as a rule very independent and are notoriously difficult to obedience train, tending to do exactly what they want to do. If that coincides with what you want, fine. If not, hard luck. Owners of these breeds usually have great difficulty getting the dog to come when called, as he is 'busy', and does not wish to be disturbed. They also tend to be very dominant dogs, and often show very assertive behaviours whenever they come into contact with other dogs, especially if the other dog is of the same sex. This often gets them into trouble, which they don't generally seem to mind too much. They are also prone to dominant behaviours with the humans that they come into contact with, even their owners, and this again can become a real problem.

Hounds

There is a saying among dog trainers that the only thing harder to train than a **Beagle** is a **Basset**. Both of these dogs belong to the hound group. This group of dogs were developed primarily to track a quarry. Their quarry varies from rabbits to people, depending upon the breed. Once on a trail however, their determination to follow it to its end is legendary. Both of the above breeds are renowned for this behaviour, and there are many owners of both types of dog who despair of getting their dog to come back once it begins following an interesting scent. Again, these dogs tend to be very greedy, and can often be influenced by the owner with the use of food, particularly if the food is strong-smelling. **Greyhounds**, by comparison, are actually quite trainable. Although not everyone's first choice when thinking of getting a dog, those who have had one usually get another. They are very gentle dogs, particularly with people, and generally have good temperaments with other dogs. If they are brought up by responsible owners, they are not, as people often say, natural cat and small dog killers. Even ex-racing greyhounds can often be homed on to pet owners who never have trouble with them attacking cats, though of course this can happen. If you take on a rescued greyhound, you should be cautious until its temperament can be ascertained.

The **Basenji**, another hound, is very unusual among dogs in that it doesn't bark. Instead, it emits sounds varying from a soft mewling to a growling noise. Another unusual character-istic of this breed is that, like wolves, the females only come into season once a year. They were bred to drive game into hunter's nets, and usually wore bells on their collars to make more noise to frighten prey. They were used to hunt and kill vermin. Although they are usually very affectionate towards people, they are not generally very friendly towards other dogs.

The **Afgan Hound** was developed to hunt gazelle, wolves and snow leopards. They tend to be independent and aloof dogs, with boundless energy. They are best known for their fabulously flowing coats. They do not stay that way without a great deal of grooming, and anyone considering buying one should be prepared to spend hours grooming it. This is another breed not known for its trainability.

Utility dogs

The utility group of dogs comprises breeds that don't quite fit into the five other Kennel Club groups – the working dogs, the gundogs, the toy dogs, the terriers and the hounds. The **Dalmation** is one of the many breeds that fall into this group. It is certainly one of the most striking breeds, and used to be called the 'plum pudding dog', for obvious reasons. It was developed to run alongside carriages in the nineteenth century. Although originally of good temperament, recently it seems to have become more nervous and more prone to aggression than it had been previously. This is perhaps due to unscrupulous breeders, particularly puppy farmers mass breeding to meet demand.

The **Poodle** was originally bred as a water dog, with a thick, corded coat. Its unusual coat helped it cut through the water. It has been used as a police dog and a retriever, and was even crossed with the Labrador to create a guide dog that didn't moult. It is generally of very good temperament, and extremely intelligent. If it has a problem, it is that it can be a little vocal.

There are several behaviours that are genetic and will be passed from generation to generation. Some of them, such as schizophrenia, can skip several generations and occur many generations later, especially if both parents have it in their ancestry. There are also behaviours that are more likely to be linked directly to observations made by puppies after they were born. I think that one of the most common is fear of strangers. In my opinion, this is not necessarily passed genetically from the mother and father. What is more likely is that the puppies pick this behaviour up from their mother after they are born.

Picture this scenario. The puppies are one week old. The doorbell rings and Mum shoots up out of her bed, displacing puppies everywhere and giving them a terrible fright. She starts to bark angrily, frightening the puppies even more. Then the door opens and a stranger enters the room. The puppies do not recognize the smell of the person, and Mum is still obviously agitated, and is perhaps removed from the room. Then this stranger starts picking the puppies up. They are still quite stressed, not really understanding what is going on. After a while the stranger leaves, and Mum returns and immediately begins washing the puppies.

This process is repeated dozens of times, and each time Mum behaves in the same way. How long would it be before the puppies learn to recognize that strangers upset their mother? If they upset her, then of course they should be upset too. The owner of the new puppy then finds at four to six months old, their puppy starts to show fear-based tendencies towards strangers.

When you look at a puppy's development from this perspective, it becomes easy to see why it is not usually a good idea to buy your puppy from a pet shop. They are very unlikely to have any knowledge of the parentage of the puppies that they sell. Most will have acquired the dogs from a puppy farm, or from an agent who takes dogs from puppy farms and sells them to the pet shop. No one can tell you anything about the parents. It is therefore a real gamble taking on one of these puppies, as there is little if any indication as to its early experiences.

Some predatory behaviour may have been learned by the dog before you buy it. Many people run from their puppy and encourage it to chase them as a game. However, if you play this game, it is quite possible that the dog will grow up believing that it is acceptable to chase people such as joggers or running children. Some find it amusing to let their puppies or young dogs chase other animals such as cats and squirrels, believing that the dog will never succeed in catching one. But I have had many distressed owners contact me whose dogs have finally caught and killed a cat or a squirrel. By then it is often too late to stop this most unpleasant behaviour.

So, to sum up:

1   Learn as much as you can about what the breed you are considering was designed to do. This behaviour could well be the most predominant characteristic in your dog's temperament. If you do not take this into account, you may be sorry later on.
2   Try to get your puppy from a reputable breeder, where you are given an opportunity to meet at least the mother and hopefully the father as well. Assessing their temperaments may give you some useful information about how the puppies will turn out. If you get one from a pet shop, it will probably have come from a puppy farm. This means that there will be no information available about the puppy's parents. Puppy farms are notorious for supplying forged pedigree papers, so the documents you get may well not be genuine anyway. The Kennel Club can be

contacted for a list of breeders for every registered breed of dog. Their details are under *Useful Addresses*.

3   If a breeder refuses to let you meet the parent or parents of a puppy because they do not like strangers, *do not buy the puppy*. It will already have learnt that behaviour from them. There will undoubtedly be times that you will want strangers to come into your house, and your dog won't.

4   Consider getting a dog from a rescue centre. There are three main advantages. Firstly you will be taking on a dog that needs help. Secondly, it is a good place to go to see many different types of dogs all in the same place, which may help you decide which type is best for you. Thirdly, as most rescue centres will have kept the dog for a while before rehoming it, it will have been observed and handled by people who are very experienced in recognizing problems in dogs and putting these problems right.

2   Dogs and Children

The type of dog that you choose when looking for a 'family dog' really depends on your individual circumstances, the children's ages, and their ability to understand the requirements of a dog. If they are very young, you must think about their way of handling what may appear to them to be a new toy. Will they be careful, or perhaps too rough? A small animal might object to this. Find out if your child is allergic to specific fur – you can do this by visiting friends with dogs to see if the children react badly to any of them. You will also need to consider the size a prospective dog will be when fully grown. Small dogs sometimes find children intimidating, and so are not always the best choice. If you are taking on a rescue dog, you should find out what it is like with children *before* you buy it.

Some dogs can be aggressive towards children. This will usually be due to unpleasant experiences it will have had with a child or children in the past. Sometimes, dogs can become very anxious about the arrival of a new baby. This usually happens with dogs that have been very close to their owners, perhaps having been 'babied' themselves. They then resent the baby getting the attention that was previously reserved for them.

The other time that you may see aggression towards the baby is when it starts crawling. Often dogs that are not used to babies will be all right with a new born, as the dog can get away from it. But once the baby can move independently, the dog becomes a thing of great interest. The baby follows the dog around the house, and suddenly the dog realizes that it has no further means of escape. Eventually the baby catches up with the dog, or perhaps climbs onto the dog while it is sleeping. The dog then growls at the baby, and is immediately punished by the owners who, understandably, want to ensure that the dog *never* reacts aggressively towards the baby. But at least, from the dog's point of view, the baby was removed.

Every time that the baby approaches the dog, the owner growls a warning at the dog not to hurt the baby. But often, telling the dog off increases the dog's resentment of the child. This is because he knows that any time that the child comes near him, he gets told off. His solution is to make sure that the baby stays away by growling.

But you have taught him not to growl a warning at the child anymore, so the dog often chooses the other option. He endures for as long as he can – then he bites! The bite is often not hard, indeed it frequently doesn't break the skin. It is a bite designed to tell the baby in no uncertain terms to leave it alone, which it does in exactly the same way that it would to a puppy or other dog that was irritating it. Understandably, the owner goes absolutely wild, and in some cases has the dog rehomed, or even destroyed. The owner believes the dog has bitten the baby 'for no reason'.

Case History – What's worse than *one* angry shepherd?

A man contacted me to discuss the situation he had at home with his family and his dogs. The man was married and had two children: a daughter, who was fifteen, and a boy of twelve. The family also had two Belgian Shepherd dogs, both male. They were both two years old, although they came from different litters.

The main reason for contacting me was because, although both dogs were showing aggression towards people in general, one of the dogs was directing most of this violent behaviour towards the young son. Although the dog had bitten the boy before, and had previously drawn blood, it was the most recent attack that prompted them to call me.

One morning, as the boy was passing the parent's bedroom on his way to the toilet, one of the dogs shot out of the parent's room and attacked him. Although the boy tried to defend himself, the dog managed to get hold of him by the neck. By the time the parents got to them and got the dog off, the boy had been badly bitten, and needed twelve stitches in his throat.

In spite of this, the parents wanted to keep the dog. They were hoping I would be able to advise them on methods of changing the dog's behaviour so that they would not have to have it destroyed. To be perfectly honest, I was not sure that this was a good idea. Although I thought that it was possible to change the dog's attitude, I could not guarantee that there would not be another biting incident for the time it would take to cure it. This was my dilemma: should I risk the son's life to save the dog, or should I ensure the son's safety by recommending that the dog be put to sleep? I felt that I had little choice, and advised them to have the dog put to sleep. They said that they could not do that without trying to help the dog get over his dislike of the boy, and asked me again to help them. Somewhat hesitantly, I agreed.

As for the other dog, although he was not exactly friendly, and didn't want to be touched by strangers, he could at least be trusted not to bite anyone unless he was provoked. He was also the more dominant of the two, and frequently put the other one in his place just for the sake of it.

All of the acts of aggression were centred around the parent's bedroom. Even the daughter would be growled at if she entered the room while the dogs were in there. So the first thing I did was pass a rule that the dogs were no longer allowed upstairs under any circumstances. The one that was most aggressive was to be kept on a long line, so that, if the dog was lying in the boy's way, he would never have to move it physically or step over it. Both of these instances had in the past caused the dog to react aggressively.

The children were now to take a much more active role in the day-to-day providing for the dogs. This would mean that they were now responsible for providing all of the things that the dogs looked forward to in a day. The son would always be responsible for feeding them. He would be the one who gave them most of their treats, and he would be the only one to give their favourite treats. He would supply their favourite toys too, so all toys had to be picked up and were never left lying around. They would only get them when he chose to let them have them. The dogs would never be given attention on demand, so they learned to appreciate attention from people much more, as they were no longer able to control it.

Neither dog would be allowed to lead a person through a doorway, and if either did, it would be brought back, so the dogs never felt that they were leading the people. They were also no longer allowed on the furniture. The best resting areas were now reserved for the people. All these measures helped to lower the dogs' status.

Because both dogs pulled badly on the lead, and neither child was strong enough to walk them, I could not have the children take them out for walks. But I could get them to produce the leads and put them on the dogs. Once we started working on curing the pulling, which went very well, we were then able to get the children to actually take the dogs out.

These dogs had many privileges – and undoubtedly it was these that had caused the aggression. The dogs had far too high a status within the pack as they saw it, therefore felt entitled to punish the children for any act which they felt threatened their positions. By doing all of these things, we lowered their rank to such a degree that there has never been any aggression from either dog since we began, even several years later.

While it is completely understandable that an owner may not want to keep a dog that they feel is a threat to their family, sometimes it helps to look at the situation from the dog's perspective. For example, imagine you were frightened of spiders, and a spider not much smaller than you were, followed you around the house. You had no means of escaping it, someone threatened you every time that you tried to chase it away, and forced you to endure it actually climbing on you. How long would it be before you reacted aggressively towards the spider? And when you did react, unlike the dog, you may well have struck to kill.

A dog will usually give several warnings before it bites. Some of those warnings will be obvious, some less so, but it will usually bite only when it feels that that is the option most likely to get the result it wants, and often only after it has tried several others. For example, if you have a dog that is nervous of babies and a baby is crawling towards it, the dog may get up and walk away. But the child follows it, so the dog learns very quickly that it cannot use that as a means of escape. So it will walk to the owners and stand by them, hoping that they will protect it. But they laugh at the way the baby follows the dog, so that doesn't work either.

The dog leaves the room, but the baby follows it there too. So finally it growls, and everything changes. The owners rush over and shout at the dog, perhaps even hitting him. But the result is that they pick up the baby and take him away. Some dogs will hate what has happened and never do it again; some dogs will learn that this is the only way to get the owners to move the baby. The punishment they received was not so unpleasant that they would not endure it again to keep the baby away. So they growl again next time, with the same result. But the owners get more aggressive, as it seems to be getting worse, and the dog's resentment of the child increases, as he now associates the baby with unpleasantness. He becomes more aggressive, and the cycle goes on until something disastrous happens.

If only the owners had recognized the potential problem and dealt with it before it got out of hand. For instance, they could have provided the dog with an escape route, perhaps a baby gate, and taught the dog to jump it, so that he knows that if the baby becomes too much, he can at least get away to a place where the child cannot follow.

Do not allow your child to climb all over your dog, pulling it and stepping on it. Regardless of how you may feel, this is probably not fun for the dog. All too often I have heard people say how good their dog is because he lets the kids do anything to him: they pull his fur and his tail, stick fingers in his ears, and dress him up in their clothes, and he never turns a hair. I would ask the owner why on earth *should* he have to endure that kind of treatment. And just because he *has* put up with it, you cannot be sure that he always will. Like us, dogs seem to have days when they are just not in the mood, and a child pulling at them may be just enough to make them lose their temper, with disastrous results. What I always find ironic is that many of these parents would never put up with a child doing to them the things that they expect the dog to endure.

Most importantly, take the time to teach your children how to handle their dog correctly. It could one day prevent a nasty injury. Many children have been snapped at by a dog, not because it is vicious, but because it reacted when it was either jumped on or had its tail stood upon whilst it was asleep!

Case History – Who's afraid of the big, bad kid?

Sam the Lurcher was afraid of children. He wasn't nervous, or apprehensive, or hesitant. He was just plain scared. The sight of a child under twelve would have him hiding behind his owner's legs emitting a low growling if he was on the lead, and running away if he was off it. Inevitably, Sam didn't spend much time off the lead. The cause of Sam's fear went back to his puppyhood, when a child had burst a balloon in his face. Although he was now fine with balloons, he was still far from fine with kids.

The first stage of getting him over his fear was to improve

his recall, so that his owners could reliably call him to them, or away from anything that might be making him stressed. We started by teaching him to respond immediately to his name. They began by playing this game, first of all with Sam close by. They armed themselves with some of his favourite titbits without him knowing that they had them. I told them to use the lowest value food that would obtain the desired behaviour. That way they would be able to save the higher value food treats for the more difficult parts of the exercise. While he was relaxed, and not paying them any particular attention, one of the owners called his name. As soon as he looked at them, they were to offer him a titbit. This process was to be repeated many times a day. Once he *always* responded immediately, it could be repeated with the dog further away, until his owners could achieve it from another room. They then moved to calling him from different parts of the house.

We also attached a sound to the reward: a whistle, so that when his owners began practising this in the park, they could use the whistle over a greater distance than their voices would carry.

Sometimes the dog had a greater incentive to stay where he was rather than return to them, so occasionally they offered a bigger reward than at other times, so that he would always think that it was worth coming back to see what was on offer. So, for example, instead of offering a single titbit between two fingers, they might be holding a whole box of treats. They were not to give him all of the treats – the trick was to let him think that they might. It was very important that the owners verbally and physically praised the dog *just before* they gave the titbits, so that in the future they could stop using the food and just use verbal praise if they wished. If the food is given before the praise, the dog is so busy with the food that it doesn't notice the verbal reward at all, and so only ever focuses on the food.

If you use food rewards in a dog's training, always remember that dogs are much more excited by foods that smell nice than foods that don't smell strong but taste nice. In some situations you may find that he would rather play than eat, so don't be afraid to offer a toy as a reward instead of food. But remember, a reward is only a reward if the dog wants it, so make it irresistible. Once the dog has the toy, he is controlling the game, and you have nothing with which to keep his attention. So teach him to play exciting tugging games with a toy like a ball on a rope, but never let him have the toy. Either you both have it or you have it. And if you are using food, remember that you need to have a quantity of food in your hand, otherwise he will take the treat and then start barking again. Use the rest of the food to keep his attention after each piece that you give him. If you have a dog that is much stronger than you are, and won't release the toy when told to, you can still play these games. All you need is a way of getting the dog to let go of the toy on command. To do this you can either use a taste deterrent put into the dog's mouth while giving the command to leave, or you can use a sound deterrent as described on p.177.

The next stage was to move on to practising this in the garden at times when there were more distractions, and again be prepared to step up the reward for the correct behaviour, perhaps using a higher value food treat. Once he progressed to a point where he could be relied upon to come when called with a lot of distractions, they started to do the same exercise at busier times, or in busier places. When he did it reliably, they then began to reduce the number of food rewards, replacing them with verbal and physical ones, but always gave him some form of reward.

To ensure that Sam responded reliably to all commands, we also needed to attach a consequence to ignoring his owners. We used the sound deterrent described on p.177.

After practising the recall exercise in the earlier paragraph, Sam became obsessed with trying to obtain that food, and nothing was more important to him. Once he was obsessed, the owners started to take him out with them on walks, and used food to eliminate his fear of children. They did this by teaching him to associate these children with something fantastic – his favourite food. At the moment that he *saw* a child, not when he began to behave fearfully, they produced the food and used it to keep his attention as they moved him away from the child. This had to be done at the moment that he first laid eyes on the child for it to work. After a while, he got to a point where he would take the sight of a child as a signal to interact with his owner instead of panicking. Once he could be reliably recalled, and didn't become stressed at the sight of a child, his owners could occasionally, say one exposure in ten, replace the food with another, lesser reward, such as a pat on the head or verbal praise. Eventually they phased the food out altogether. This process had to be used every time that he was walked in a place where he might encounter a child, until he was cured. They could then walk him anywhere they chose.

If you are planning a baby, make sure that you have not made your dog so much of a substitute child that it will be jealous of the real one. Even if you have, you can still do something about it. Start to break down some of the obsessive bonds that have been created with the dog *well before* the baby arrives. Move the dog from the bedroom, as the dog may resent the arrival of a new baby in his sleeping area. Start to get the dog used to the sounds and smells of babies, and to associate them with something pleasant. Record the sound of different babies crying on an audio tape and play it in situations where the dog would normally be happy, at meal times or just before going on a walk. This will teach him to regard the baby as a source of something pleasurable. Place his dinner bowl on a mat or piece of towel, and sprinkle baby powder or a little baby oil on to the towel. Put a little on your hands just before getting his lead, so that he smells baby smells at these times. Perhaps even bathe yourself in baby bath, so that you smell like your baby.

Get hold of a life-like doll and practise feeding, dressing and playing with it. Let the dog get used to these things happening long before the baby arrives. You can even put the doll in the baby's cot or pram with the crying tape in it, so it sounds as though the doll itself is crying and respond to it exactly the way you would with your real baby when it arrives.

In summary, if you already have a dog and a child and you are having problems, you need to contact a behaviourist as soon as possible. If you have a dog, are planning to start a family and are worried about how the dog will take to a new addition to his pack, remember that your dog has been an important part of your life, loyal and devoted, and does not deserve to be put on the shelf because of your new arrival.

1 Try to make time for him too. Find the time to play with him and walk him and do all of the things that you used to do. If possible, do them after you play with the baby, so that the dog is aware that, although it is still loved, it is nonetheless last in the pack order. This is especially important with a dog that shows dominant tendencies.

2 Try to prepare the dog by breaking down any obsessive

bonds that may have formed between you and the dog, well before the baby arrives. For example, remove the dog from the bedroom and furniture. Do not carry the dog like a baby if the dog is small. Do not constantly respond to the dog's demands for attention.

3   Use the washing and bathing products that you will be using on your baby. That way the dog will become used to those smells, and your baby won't smell so strange to him.

4   Find a realistic toy, carry it around and do all of the things with it that you would do with a real baby, to get the dog used to it. If the dog attacks it as soon as your back is turned, you will know that you have real problems ahead, and you should contact a behaviourist *immediately*.

5   Tape the sound of different babies crying and play the tape throughout the day, particularly at times when the dog is happy.

6   If you are not prepared to continue to treat the dog as a valued member of the family, then perhaps he *is* better off in a new home.

3 How Many Dogs Are Too Many Dogs?

One of the first calls that I attended as an animal welfare officer involved a single mother of two living in a tiny council flat. She had very little money, and almost no furniture. She also owned a Rottweiler and a Dachshund cross. As a means of making herself some extra cash, she had decided to acquire a Rottweiler bitch, which she planned to mate to the dog and later sell the puppies. This she did, but decided to keep one puppy, the largest male, for herself. When she contacted me, she was on the verge of a breakdown, as between the two children under five, and the four dogs, she was, not surprisingly, finding it hard to cope. When I visited her, I advised her that it might be in the best interests of both her two- and four-footed family members that some of the dogs were rehoused. She agreed, and signed all four dogs over to the animal welfare for rehoming.

This story may sound unbelievable, but I have come across many cases of owners who have brought more than one dog for the wrong reasons, and paid a price for their error in judgement.

Case History – Too many chiefs . . .

A woman who owned four West Highland White Terriers contacted me, as she was having real problems with her dogs. Originally, she had only had one, a male. He was two years old, and fancied himself as a bit of a ladies' man. He had begun to make himself a nuisance in the local park, where he would consider almost every dog to be a potential mate, regardless of the other dog's feelings on the subject.

So his owner decided to get him some company, thinking that if he had his own bitch, he would feel less inclined to pursue others. Wrong! Although he showed little interest in the new puppy, he continued in his relentless pursuit of other more suitable companions.

The owner now had to deal with the responsibility of training a puppy, as well as controlling her older dog. As time went by and the bitch puppy reached adulthood, the owner decided to breed from the pair. So she mated them. Not surprisingly, the dog was more than happy to oblige.

In time she produced a litter of five puppies. The owner decided to keep one of the puppies, a bitch. And then there were three. The three seemed to get on well at first, with just minor squabbles between the two bitches as the puppy got older and began to challenge her mother. However, as time went by, the arguments between them got worse, with ever-greater aggression being used. The dog stayed out of these battles, and no one seemed to want to pick a fight with him. He was now six, and although he was still very interested in strange dogs, especially bitches, his advances towards the bitches in his household had waned almost to extinction.

Then the owner got a call from a woman who had taken in one of the litter. It seemed that the bitch that she had bought had not settled in very well, and was not trustworthy with the children, so she had decided that the dog would have to go. The breeder volunteered to have the dog back.

When the dog arrived, the two resident bitches were rather less than welcoming. The new bitch immediately started a fight with her mother, and the other sister leapt to her mother's defence. The owner broke up the fight, put the mother in another room with the original sister, and decided to try again, this time putting the new bitch in with the dog. This pairing seemed to work much better, the dog was his usual amorous self with a new lady, and she was suitably flirtatious.

These two quickly became inseparable, and ate, slept and played together. The new bitch was given limited, supervised access to the other two bitches, and, gradually, an uneasy alliance was formed between them. It soon became clear that the new bitch wanted to rule over the other females, and the owner decided that she would allow this to happen, as the new bitch had the full backing of the dog, and the pair seemed to control things most of the time anyway.

Once the new bitch was allowed access to where the other two bitches lived, she started spending a lot of her time sleeping in her sister's bed. The sister was clearly not happy about this, but had lost enough confidence over the months to know not to challenge the new addition. Once she was sure that she had dominated her sister, the new dog then started work on her mother. This proved harder, and fights often ensued, but with the backing of the dog, the young bitch invariably came out on top, and finally the mother gave in too.

Inevitably, things didn't stop there. The owner rang me at the point where the bitch had actually begun to challenge the dog. She had started sleeping in his bed, and would growl if he approached it which always resulted in a fight. She would muscle in whenever the owner stroked him or tried to play with him. If she couldn't stop this happening, she would attack the dog, and again a fight would ensue. The fights between these two were always difficult to break up, and the owner was finding it increasingly stressful. To add to this, the young bitch would no longer allow either of the two other bitches any interaction with the dog. She was also liable to attack them if the owner paid them any attention, so if the owner wished to stroke or groom them, she had to put the young bitch outside the room.

Really, the main problem here was that the owner had failed to recognize the potential for problems in taking on more dogs, dogs that she hadn't really wanted in the first place. She had also failed to make it clear to the dogs what the pack order was. It fluctuated in different situations, and this caused confusion between the dogs.

Stopping the aggression between the two dogs was not too difficult. First we had to elevate the owner's position so that she was better able to influence the behaviour of the dogs. Then we had to make it clear to the bitch that the dog was higher ranked than she was. So, the dog was allowed to sleep upstairs in the hallway, it was always fed first, nearer to where the owner sat when she ate, and had its lead put on and taken off first. It was always stroked first, and the owner was told to use a sound deterrent (see p.177) if the bitch tried to approach while the dog was getting attention. The owner also made it clear that the young bitch was second-in-command, and she got everything second. Although she was still allowed to rank higher than the other bitches, she was no longer allowed to punish them.

Undoubtedly, there can be advantages to having more than one dog. Food can be bought in greater bulk, so it can sometimes work out almost as cheap to feed two dogs as it is to feed one. They can be good company for each other, though this depends upon the temperament of the individual dogs. They can give each other a great deal of exercise. And if one dies, you will not be left without a dog at all.

There are also disadvantages to having a second dog. It can mean that there is a potential doubling of any problems. There can be twice the fouling, twice the destruction, and twice the barking. You could incur twice the kennelling fees when the family go on holiday. You may also face the dilemma of what to do if the two dogs don't get on. Many people then find it difficult to rehome one of the dogs, so have to find elaborate ways of keeping the dogs apart, as they come to dislike each other so much that they cannot even be kept in the same room together. Two dogs will often compete against each other to find out who will be 'top dog', so they do things like pull badly on the lead, as they both want to be in front of the other. The owner often makes this situation worse by promoting different dogs in different situations. For example, when it comes to feeding time, they will feed the oldest dog, which promotes him as the leader. Then when it comes to taking the dogs out for a walk, they put the young dog's lead on first and allow him to be in front walking down the road, which promotes him, and obviously confuses the dogs as to what the pack status really is.

But possibly the biggest mistake that people make in getting a second dog is that they don't take enough time to consider whether or not the first dog actually wants a second dog at all. The owner assumes that, because he gets on really well with other dogs in the park, he would like to live with another dog. But in reality he is a pack animal, and has worked out exactly where he fits in. Dogs are also quite jealous animals, and often won't appreciate the competition for the owner's attentions. So before you get another dog, perhaps you could try to find a dog that he gets on well with, and ask the owner if they would mind you looking after him for a week, perhaps if they go on holiday. If they agree, bring him over to your house and see how they get on. Make sure that his owners are aware that if it doesn't work out, you will return him to his own house and look after him there until they return.

Some people end up with too many dogs for all the wrong reasons.

Case History – Did he help or hinder?

A case that I was recently told of concerned a man living in a two-bedroom flat, who had been given a dog by a rescue centre. He had fostered dogs for them before, and he was asked to look after this dog until a suitable home could be found. The dog had a few minor behavioural problems, and it was felt by the centre that some time spent in a house would prepare the dog for rehoming and therefore improve its chances.

After two months, it became clear that finding a home for the dog was proving more difficult than the rescue centre had thought. The keeper had by this time grown very attached to the dog, so decided to keep him. The centre was happy to let him, and so the dog stayed where it was.

Soon afterwards, the centre contacted him to ask if he was prepared to take on a second dog. This dog had come from the same address as the first, so the two dogs knew each other. Although the second dog was a bitch, she had been speyed, so there was no risk of puppies. The man agreed, and the bitch arrived.

Everything was fine, until a few months later the home asked the man if he could temporarily look after two more dogs. These two were a male and female who were said to get on well with other dogs, so the home felt that there shouldn't be any problems. Although they were also opposite sexes, the male had been neutered. The man accepted the dogs. Needless to say, it was not long before the inevitable happened, and the un-castrated male got to the un-speyed bitch. The result was seven puppies.

As the man was worried about the puppies picking up any diseases from the adult dogs, he stopped walking the adults in the park, where he felt that they were most at risk. Instead he only walked them around the streets.

One day, the man returned from a trip to the local shops to find that he had left his keys indoors, and had no means of getting in. The dogs were barking very loudly, and only got worse as the owner pushed and pulled at the door. While he was standing on the doorstep trying to figure out what to do next, the police arrived with an RSPCA inspector. One of his neighbours had reported him, alleging that he had eleven dogs living in squalid conditions, and that the dogs were barking in a distressed manner and had been for some time.

The police broke into the flat, and the RSPCA inspector seized the dogs. The man was prosecuted and summoned to appear in court. The defence argued that indeed the house was far from tidy, and that there would be no way that it would have been acceptable to bring up a child in such conditions. However, there is no evidence to prove that a dog mentally suffers as a result of living in an untidy house. It was also argued that the owner had acted in the dogs' best interests by not taking them to the park, and this had only been intended to be for a short time until the puppies had been rehomed. Unfortunately, the whole case took over a year to be resolved. This meant that the puppies, all of whom had been kept in kennels for the duration as evidence were by now suffering serious behavioural problems, and two of the puppies were put to sleep, as it was felt that they could not be safely homed because of their temperaments. Ironically, it was only through being kennelled for so long that they had developed temperament problems in the first place. The remaining dogs were returned to the owner.

What had happened here was that in his efforts to help the dogs, the owner had overlooked the responsibility of having that number of dogs in a very small flat. He had not considered the disturbance they might cause to neighbours, nor the difficulty of keeping the male and female apart when she inevitably came into season. In hindsight, I would question the responsibility of the rescue centre for giving him the dogs in the first place, as he clearly had insufficient room to separate them. At the very least, they should have neutered either one or better still both of them to prevent an unwanted pregnancy.

So if you are thinking about getting another dog:

1   Think carefully about whether or not you can afford to pay potentially double the cost of everything that you currently pay for with only one dog.

2   Be sure that everyone in the family really wants another dog, and if anyone doesn't, will it be fair on them or the dog to get one anyway?
3   If you already have a dog, stop and think if that dog will really want to share everything that he currently thinks of as belonging to *him*.

4 A Member of the Family?

For many people, the family dog is a highly valued friend. For some he is a surrogate child. For others he represents a figure that can have all of the owner's love and attention lavished upon him, in the absence of any human partner. There are those for whom their dog stands for all of these things and more. They love him and he loves them! Or does he?

Certainly, he seems to show a lot of human characteristics, which is partly why we are so close to our dogs. But is it a good idea to humanize them too much? Trying to make our dogs too human causes a lot of the problems that behaviourists are called upon to help put right. Also, owners often end up feeling let down by their dogs, because the dog seems ungrateful for all they have done for it. This then builds up resentment towards the dog. In reality, the owner has forgotten that, regardless of how intelligent he may seem, or how his eyes look almost human sometimes, he is still nothing more than a dog. Perhaps an exceptional dog, but a dog nonetheless. Attributing human characteristics and status to him will almost invariably lead to problems for the dog, the owner or both.

Many of the owners that request a visit from me are people who have raised their dog's status to the point where it equals or exceeds their own (at least in the dog's opinion). Some of the consequences of this can be very serious. Taking over areas such as the owner's bed and not allowing them access to it, not allowing people near the area in which it is feeding, not allowing itself to be touched, stealing and using aggression to keep the thing it stole even though it obviously doesn't really want it. These are just a few of the things dogs use to demonstrate their power within a household. Not very acceptable behaviour for a 'member of the family'!

Case History – It's my house!

I was recently asked for help from a man who was having major problems with his dog, a 4-year-old Labrador/Boxer cross. The problem, the owner told me over the phone, was that the dog was very aggressive towards other dogs.

When I arrived at the door and rang the bell, the door opened a crack. 'Just hold on a second please, Robert,' I was told. 'Sit, sit, come on now sit, good boy Tyson, sit, sit, sit down, ah ah ah sit Tyson. Good dog, now stay, stay Tyson, stay, AH AH AH AH STAY Tyson stay, OKAY ROBERT, COME IN QUICKLY!'

As soon as I came through the door I found myself wearing a Labrador/Boxer coat – extra large. This enormous, slavering beast grabbed me by the arm and dragged me up the hallway, seemingly non-aggressively, but giving me little time to refuse his invitation to come in. 'Oh, he obviously likes you,' exclaimed his owner. 'If he didn't, he'd be growling.' This, however, did little to reassure me of Tyson's good intentions.

All the way to the living-room, I was besieged by this delinquent dog, pulling at my arms and clothes, and trying to bite my feet as I walked. Finally we reached the living-room and I sat down. The dog was immediately climbing onto my lap. 'TYSON, GET DOWN!' said his owner. 'DOWN, GET DOWN, TYSON DOWN!' I think I had more chance of winning Miss World than he had of getting the dog off me. Before I could take steps to remove the dog myself, it decided that it would move on to trying to steal my pen. So began a game of 'chase the pen'. No matter where I hid it, the dog would try to get to it. When this failed, he decided to try to get the hand holding the pen instead. This went on for several minutes before the dog got tired and had to take a momentary breather. It spied a book on the table so took that and, lying down, began to tear it to pieces. 'Well, that'll keep him occupied for a while,' said his owner. 'He loves tearing paper.'

I asked the owner what, apart from the obvious, were his problems. 'Well, he hates other dogs, he attacks sheep and horses, he steals anything he can get his teeth on, he chases cars, he bites everyone that comes to the house the way he did to you, though we don't seem to get many visitors nowadays. He pulls very badly on the lead, my wife can no longer walk him and he never gets let off the lead anymore as he won't come back when called, he fouls indoors and he despises cats. He grabs hold of things that he knows he shouldn't and will not let go, regardless of what we say or do. We tried throwing bunches of keys at him, but he then takes the keys and won't give them back. So we have to offer him food to make him drop them. I know that he sounds terrible, but apart from all of that, he is a really lovely dog,' the owner emphasized.

Here was an example of a dog that had been given far too much power over his owners by them treating him as a member of the family – a substitute child. What they had overlooked was that dogs do not have the same sense of appreciation for being well treated as humans do. In fact, most dogs simply see owners like him as weak leaders, and they then try to take over the running of the pack. This doesn't mean that Tyson was a bad dog. It simply means that he was a confused one, not sure what the rules were and how to follow them correctly. So he had decided that the best way forward was to make his own rules, and teach everyone to follow them.

Case History – When three's definitely a crowd

A case that a colleague of mine told me of involved a male Shih Tzu that was bought as a present for his wife. He worked on an oil rig, and so was away from home for long periods. Time went by, and the third time the husband returned home from the rig he found that things at home had changed somewhat. The dog had basically taken over the role of the dominant male, and saw the husband as a rival for his territory and his mate – the wife! He found that the dog would not allow him to sit on any chair that the wife was already occupying,

and would get in between them and growl menacingly at the husband until he moved.

At meal times, the dog had his own place at the table, and incredibly, when food was put on the table, the dog would walk past his food, and past the wife's until he reached the husband's plate. He would then eat a portion of the husband's food, making it clear that this was his right as the pack leader, and would then return to his own plate and commence eating. At night the husband was only allowed into the bedroom and into the bed providing he got there BEFORE the wife and the dog got in there. Otherwise the dog would attack him and drive him from the room. Even then the dog would sleep in between them, and play gooseberry all night. This again was a dog that had been granted too high a status by the wife, who had tried to make the dog a replacement for the family she didn't have.

In summary:

1   As much as you may and indeed should love your dog, never forget that that is all that he is. He is not human, even though he may seem to be at times. He is not governed by the same rules of behaviour as we are, and it is a mistake to treat him as though he is. In doing this we run the risk of trying to turn him into a substitute human, which he can never be, and he will invariably suffer in the long run if his owner tries to make him behave as if he were.

2   If you have more than one dog, make sure that they are all aware of where they fit in to the pack structure. If this is clear, you are much less likely to be faced with dogs trying to work their way up the pack through challenging you or each other.

3   If your dog behaves in a dominant manner (see under

Aggression), do not allow him to get away with doing things that will further convince him that he is higher ranked than you are, such as lying on furniture, sleeping in your bedroom or eating at the table.

5 Good Health

Nothing is more important than the health of both ourselves and our pets. In order to keep our dogs healthy we must feed, exercise, vaccinate and worm them, as well as keeping them clean and well groomed. By doing all of these things we will be doing a great deal to ensure that our dogs remain in good health.

But there is still the chance of an unforeseen accident or illness occurring, and you should take this into consideration when you decide to have a dog, and when choosing the breed.

Unfortunately there is no National Health Service for animals, and serious accident or illness can cost hundreds or even thousands of pounds in vet bills. There are charity organisations such as the RSPCA, PDSA and the Blue Cross which may be able to help you if you can't afford private vet fees, but these should not be relied upon in the first instance because you may not qualify for help. These services are frequently duped into treating animals who belong to people who could afford to go to a private vet, so some of them have tightened up regulations about who can be seen. As charities, they have budgets that make very difficult demands on them.

One way to reduce the cost of your vet bills is to take out a pet insurance policy. You pay a monthly premium, and your pet is then covered against the majority of illnesses or accidents.

Hygiene and grooming

Hygiene and grooming are two of the most important ways in which we can safeguard our dogs' health. Grooming gives us an opportunity to check our pets for any skin problems or parasitic infestations. It also improves the condition of the coat.

Hygiene is important, for although it is often thought that animals keep themselves as clean as they need to be, this is not always the case.

For ourselves, it is most important to wash our hands after we have handled animals. Bearing in mind where a dog's tongue goes, they should not be allowed to lick our hands or faces.

Vaccinations

Puppies should be vaccinated for the first time when they are about nine weeks old (this can vary according to the type of vaccine your particular vet uses). As puppies, they will require a course of two to three injections over a few weeks, and after that they will require a yearly booster injection. If you acquire a dog and you are not sure whether it has been vaccinated, it is best to assume that it has not, and start again with the set of puppy injections.

The diseases that dogs are vaccinated against are:

leptospirosis, distemper, parvovirus and adenovirus (canine hepatitis). Vets can also vaccinate against kennel cough, but this is rarely done for two reasons. Firstly, there are numerous types of kennel cough, and the vaccines available do not prevent them all. Secondly, although very contagious, it is only fatal if a second illness takes hold because the dog is run down from kennel cough. This however is very rare, so all in all it is not recommended as strongly as the other vaccinations.

Obviously all vaccines cost money, but they all protect your pets against diseases that are potentially fatal. The cost is also minimal if you compare it to the price of long-term veterinary care should your pet become ill with a preventable disease.

For those who are concerned about the risks involved in using conventional viral vaccines of the type administered by vets yearly, homeopathic vaccinations are an option. They certainly eliminate the risks associated with the standard vaccines, but there are concerns that they have not been tested on enough dogs for a long enough trial period to be sure of their effectiveness.

Parasites

It is very important to keep your pet free from parasites, as they can have an adverse effect on not only their health, but on yours also.

Fleas

Most dogs will at some time in their lives get fleas. As well as feeling very uncomfortable, many dogs are allergic to flea saliva, and terrible skin problems as well as hair loss can result. The most important thing to remember when trying either to prevent flea infestation or to solve an existing problem is that the flea only stays on the host animals for as long as it takes it to feed. Once it has filled with blood it drops into the carpet or between the floorboards to digest the meal, and there it will stay until it is ready for another feed. So it is crucial that you treat the home as well as your pet. Remember to spray your pet regularly, following the instructions carefully.

The flea's worst enemy is the vacuum cleaner, but simply being sucked up won't kill it. As soon as the vacuum is switched off they will jump back out again, so you need to spray your flea spray into the vacuum first.

Do not be tempted to buy treatments like flea sprays or worming tablets from pet shops, as they are not licensed to sell the stronger, more effective brands. Always be careful to follow the manufacturer's directions. You should never mix products as you can overdose your pet (e.g., do not flea spray a dog that is already wearing a flea collar). It can cause serious illness, even death.

Ticks

Like fleas, ticks are blood drinkers. They are usually picked up by dogs running through long grass, especially in areas where sheep graze. When they first attach themselves to the dog they are quite small, but soon swell up with the blood that they drink from the host, until they look like large grey warts. Removing them yourself can be risky, as while feeding, the ticks' head and mouth-parts are embedded beneath the dog's skin. If you pull the tick off and accidentally leave the head hooked into his skin an abscess may form. Therefore it is safest to have it removed by a vet.

Worms

Roundworms (ascarids) and tapeworms (cestodes) commonly affect our dogs. There are a few different varieties.

The most significant of the roundworms in relation to our own health is *Toxocara canis*. This worm lives in the intestine of the dog and the eggs are passed out in the faeces. The eggs can be spread for quite a distance by the wind, car wheels and the soles of shoes etc.

In the adult dog there is hardly any sign of illness at all, but in young puppies infection can cause heavy breathing, coughing, diarrhoea, vomiting, poor growth and even death.

The larval stage of the worm can be picked up by people, and children are most at risk because this stage can be ingested when unwashed hands are put into the mouth. Although rare, in some cases larvae can migrate through the bloodstream into the tissues of the eye, liver, brain or other organs and cause damage.

You can reduce this risk if you have a dog by regularly worming it with products bought *from the vet*, and by keeping your child away from heavily fouled dog areas.

There are many varieties of tapeworm that dogs can carry. These are easy to notice, as the animal usually passes out segments in which the eggs are contained. The segments look like grains of rice and can be seen in the animal's faeces or in the hair around the anal area. It is extremely rare for people to pick up tapeworm from their pet, as the worm requires an intermediate host in order to develop. It is not accepted that the greater risk comes from eating infected meat, although this type of infection is also uncommon.

It is extremely important to worm pets regularly and properly. Pregnant dogs should be wormed before the young are born, then the puppies should be wormed at two to three weeks, and ever two to three weeks after that until they leave their mothers. They should then be wormed at three months, six months, and every six months thereafter. Ensure that the product you use is effective against both roundworms and tapeworms. Sometimes it is necessary to use two separate products. Follow the instructions carefully, as it is possible to overdose your pet and cause serious illness.

You can also help to prevent the spread of worms by cleaning up after your dog has defecated, and disposing of it carefully. Dogs can be encouraged to defecate in reserved areas like dog exercise areas in parks.

Feeding

One of the major considerations to be made when acquiring a dog should be the cost of its upkeep (already outlined in Chapter 1. Obviously a Chihuahua is going to be a lot cheaper to feed than a Great Dane! Work out all the relevant finances before you start, and if the cost of food is a possible worry, do not get an inappropriate breed.

What foods give a balanced diet?

Food is directly related to health. For example, if your dog is suffering from a vitamin or mineral deficiency caused by something lacking in its diet, it may become ill, and specific deficiencies are often recognizable in the symptoms the animal is showing. Whatever type of dog you choose, a balanced diet is essential.

When it comes down to specific variations of one type of food, buying the most expensive or well-known brand does not guarantee that you have bought the best for your dog.

Many tinned foods are very rich, and not all dogs' digestive systems can cope with them. Often they are little more than offal, with an emulsifying jelly to hold them together, plus added vitamins to make up for what they lack. They also have an enormous amount of water, as much as 90 per cent in some cases. All you are really giving your dog is a meaty drink.

In an effort to stop a dog's digestive problems, owners may go from one food to another. This usually results in the animal getting worse, as its body never has a chance to adjust to one food, or the foods used are still of the wrong type. In this situation, check with your vet to make sure that there is nothing physically wrong with the dog's digestive system, and take advice from the vet about a diet to suit your dog.

If you want to change your pet's food, it is best to do so *gradually*. Add a small portion of the new type of food to his dinner, then add a little more every day until you are feeding entirely the new food. If you have had your dog checked by the vet and it is just a case of finding the correct food, you can put your dog on a diet of boiled chicken or fish (no skin or bones) and add boiled rice. This can be given for a few days until the dog's stomach calms down. You can then gradually introduce a sensible food of your choice.

Some feel that the best form of food you can give to a dog is what it would eat naturally – fresh raw meat. There certainly seems to be some logic in this, especially in view of the additives in some preparatory foods, particularly some of the dried foods. Research has shown that some of these foods contain ingredients that are not considered fit for canine consumption. Things like feathers, feet and claws, which would otherwise be thrown away, are sometimes added in the processing of some dried foods, and these are not readily digestible by dogs, but are used to make up bulk.

Dogs fed primarily on scraps often have health problems as

they rarely get a correct balance of vitamins and minerals, although if they do not have a sensitive stomach you can give them very small quantities of leftovers without causing problems.

Cooked bones should not be given, as they can splinter when chewed and lodge in the dog's throat or intestines. People still do this, believing as they have done it for years why not continue? But when there are so many safer substitutes that the dog can have, why risk serious illness, or even death?

Weight gain

If your dog is gaining weight, it is usually because it is being fed too much food and/or is not getting sufficient exercise to burn the food up.

The usual reason people give for their dog being overweight is that it has been neutered and the operation has made it fat. This is not strictly true. After being neutered, because of hormone changes in the body, an animal usually needs less food than it did before. Unaware of this, owners continue feeding the same amount of food and consequently the dog gains weight. With male dogs that have been neutered, there can actually be an increase in appetite, and owners will sometimes give in to these demands for more food. Obesity can lead to a number of problems, and arthritis and heart disease are often the end result. When an animal is fat, all the muscles in the body have to work harder to carry the extra weight about, and as the heart is a type of muscle, it too has to work harder. This may enlarge it in the same way that other muscles build up when worked hard, and this can lead to heart disease.

To over-feed your dog to the point where it is suffering in

terms of its movement or lack of energy is not only thought-less, but in my opinion actually cruel. There is nothing sadder to see than a young dog, or even an old one, plodding along behind its owner on the lead, fat and panting and feeling like the whole walk is an endurance test. Many of these dogs, given the correct amount of food and exercise, could still be very active and mobile. Not only are they unhappy, they are also at serious risk of a much shorter lifespan. As your dog gets older it will understandably start to 'slow up', so you should reduce its food accordingly as it needs less calories. If you feed a slower 12-year-old dog the same amount as you fed it when it was a 2-year-old charging around with endless energy, it *will* inevitably get fat. So be sensible, and your pet will lead a far happier life.

Weight loss

Sometimes the opposite is true and a dog is too thin. This is either due to under-feeding, over-exercising, or a medical problem.

If you feel that you are giving your pet enough food, but it is still not gaining weight, check with your vet what the correct weight should be, and inform them of the amount and type of food you are feeding. This should give them a good idea of the problem. There are specific digestive problems that are relatively common in dogs, and are more common in certain breeds.

Many illnesses can lead to weight loss, so what you shouldn't do is watch your pet gradually losing weight for a long time and only take him to the vet when he is really thin. If he is losing weight noticeably take him to be seen sooner rather than later, because you can prevent other problems by early action.

If you are concerned about choosing the correct type of food for your dog, there are a number of helpful books listed under *Recommended Reading* at the back of this book. As diet will seriously affect your dog's life and continued health, it is something that you should take as much time with as you would with your own diet, or that of your children.

Remember when reading manufacturers' guidelines on pet food that they are only guidelines, and quantities needed vary from one individual to another.

Exercise

How much exercise your dog should be given will depend on a number of factors, such as the size of the dog, its age, its weight and its health. It is often believed that the bigger the dog the more exercise it needs, but this is not always the case. For example, a Jack Russell Terrier has boundless energy and will run forever, whereas a Saint Bernard will tire quite quickly and indeed should not have a massive amount of exercise.

Sometimes people's circumstances mean that they cannot spend a great deal of time walking a dog and so they choose a small breed. However, all too often they misjudge the amount of exercise even a small dog will require. Terriers are frequently chosen because they are small, but as they have a great deal of energy and need a considerable amount of exercise, they are often owned by someone who cannot give them sufficient exercise. By contrast, very large dogs, such as Great Danes and Saint Bernards, do not need as much exercise as their size might suggest. The very short-legged, snub-nosed breeds such as the Pekingese and Lhasa Apso are generally speaking content to trot or walk beside their owners, with occasional runs. This is probably just as well, because should they run too much they might have difficulty breathing in enough air to recover as quickly as a long-nosed breed.

Dogs can become destructive through lack of exercise. For example, Border Collies, which mentally mature very quickly, and are extremely intelligent, often end up in the most unsuitable of environments, in small flats for example, with the owners out at work all day. At a very early age this dog can become bored, and it has a vast amount of nervous energy to use up from the start. These owners may well end up having their homes wrecked by a bored, frustrated dog!

If this pup was given a good run two or more times a day to wear it out, perhaps it would not exhibit this undesirable behaviour. Think carefully about what a dog has been bred for in the past. If you go out and get a Border Collie pup, instinctively he will want to herd things and generally race around. This of course takes a lot of exercise, and his feelings won't change by housing him in a small area and walking around the green. If you are not in a position to exercise him enough, don't get him – it is not fair on the dog.

When it comes to 'needs', both owner and dog should be considered.

Generally speaking, a dog's exercise requirements fluctuate throughout its life. As a very young puppy, it will become tired quite quickly and need lots of sleep. Then as it nears adulthood, it will require a lot more exercise as it will have masses of energy to burn off. As it nears old age it will begin to slow down, and as an old dog it may only want a little exercise, much as it did when a very young puppy. However, this may vary on the type of dog you have. Large breeds in particular may develop movement-related problems in later life, so it is best not to give them too much exercise as young puppies because their legs and joints need time to strengthen before they are made to work too hard. The bones of heavy breeds like Mastiffs can bend if they are allowed to run too much, especially up and down stairs, as young pups.

Recommended reading on this subject

Volhard, Wendy, and Kerry Brown DVM, *The Holistic Guide to a Healthy Dog* (Howell Book House, New York, 1995)

6 To Neuter or Not to Neuter

This is a decision that only you can make. There is no legal obligation to castrate or spay your dog or bitch, but perhaps there are moral ones.

Below are listed some of the advantages in having your dog neutered. Also listed are what people believe to be disadvantages. However, most of these are completely inaccurate.

If you have an un-neutered dog, take a few minutes to read this chapter, then make up your mind which is the best alternative for you and your dog.

Advantages to neutering	Commonly believed opinions about neutering
No unwanted or unplanned litters	She will miss not having children
No stray dogs queuing outside your house or getting into your garden hoping to mate your bitch.	She doesn't like other dogs, so there is no mating problem
My dog no longer tries to escape and look for bitches, and has stopped scent marking everywhere.	I've taken away his manhood
My bitch is unlikely to get a pyometra (a potentially fatal infection of the uterus) and less likely to get mammary cancer in later life	Her spirit was broken after she was spayed

Advantages to neutering	Commonly believed opinions about neutering
My male dog will not be at risk from testicular tumours, and it will greatly reduce the risk of prostate problems.	He will get fat
No more trying to keep my bitch in for three weeks, twice a year, with blood everywhere	She won't settle until she has had a litter
No more mounting anything that will support his weight!	It's good for him to relieve his frustration
Although neutering is expensive, there are places that run reduced rates, and it will be much cheaper than raising a litter of puppies	It is still too expensive!
Thousands of dogs are put to sleep every year because they have been picked up straying and haven't been claimed, neutering reduces the numbers	I could probably borrow the money for a fine, but he hasn't been picked up yet so they'll probably never catch him
Thousands of puppies (and kittens) are put to sleep every year because they are from unwanted litters. Neutering can prevent this	I know I'll be able to find good homes, my neighbour is having one, she didn't plan to but I managed to persuade her. My brother, sister and aunt are all very busy and they weren't looking for one either, but I talked them into it because I didn't want them going to just anybody

'If I neuter my dog, it will get fat.'

This does happen, but only because the dog gets too little exercise, or because most owners do not reduce the dog's daily food intake after neutering. It is often a combination of both. Males in particular often have an increased appetite after castration, but don't be tempted to increase the food. Hormone levels in neutered dogs and bitches change, and they burn up less calories. As a result they usually need less food. Consult with your vet about the correct amount your dog now requires.

'It is better for my bitch to let her have a litter.'

Why? If you let a boisterous dog have a litter supposedly to calm her down, you may find her just as boisterous after raising puppies. If you feel you are depriving her by not letting her have pups, speak to friends who have spayed bitches and ask if their dogs are 'suffering' because they haven't given birth. For a lot of bitches pregnancy is a very stressful, awkward time, especially if she is in a busy, noisy house where she has very little peace and quiet, and so it is probably not much fun at all.

'If I castrate my dog I will be taking away his manhood, and I wouldn't like it done to me!'

Firstly, a dog that has been castrated does not 'know' he has been done. He doesn't look between his hind legs and gasp at the loss of his manhood, as he has no true 'understanding' of the purpose his testicles serve. He does not know that their removal means he will not be able to produce sperm to fertilise a bitch's eggs. He doesn't even realize that they have gone. It can also be very frustrating for a male dog to be able to smell bitches in season and be forever denied the opportunity to mate with them. As castration eliminates this frustration it could be argued that with many dogs, particularly highly sexed ones, it is cruel *not* to have them done.

Do not make the mistake of attributing a human sense of loss to an animal that will not feel that loss, and will probably only benefit from it.

'If I castrate my aggressive dog, it will make him less aggressive towards other dogs.'

This is not necessarily true. If the dog is showing aggression towards all dogs of both sexes, towards guests in your house, or towards your other dog, castrating him may do nothing to improve his behaviour. In fact in some cases it may even make him worse. Castration will probably help with sex-related aggression, and may help with dominant aggression in conjunction with a programme of other corrective measures. For this owners should seek professional advice, either from a behaviour counsellor or someone else who has the necessary training and experience to advise on this type of problem.

'If I neuter my dog, will he stop trying to mate with cushions, the cat and people's legs?'

Yes, almost certainly, provided that he is castrated before the urge to try to mate with everything has become a habit. Once this happens, chances are that castrating him is much less likely to make a significant difference as he now does it because he knows nothing else; but this is usually only the case when the dog has done it for years.

'I should let my bitch have a litter, as I already have enough potential homes for the puppies.'

Are you sure that all the homes will be suitable and permanent? It is estimated that, out of an average litter of eight puppies, only two will live to old age in their first new home. A lot of people will take on a puppy for the wrong reasons: it looked cute; it was a present; their neighbour just happened to have some. Perhaps it is intended to keep the children occupied, or as a deterrent to thieves. But what many of these people do not consider fully is the amount of work a dog needs. As a puppy it will be destructive, and a puppy can wreak a phenomenal amount of damage in a very short time, especially if it is left alone all day while the new owners are out at work. Until it gets older it will need to be taken out after every meal, every nap and several times in between if it is to become house-trained. It is often for one or both of these reasons that a dog is put out before owners go to work in the morning, to ensure that it does not mess or chew in the house. But what happens to the dog? Chances are he will end up being run over, perhaps injuring or even killing himself and/or a member of the public in the process. He may even be picked up by a dog warden and if he is not collected he may be rehomed or put to sleep.

Therefore think seriously of breeding any puppies – they don't stay small, cute and cuddly for long, and they do need serious commitment from any new owner.

'What is a "season"?'

This is the time that a bitch becomes receptive to the advances of prospective mates. Her vulva will swell and she will begin to discharge small amounts of blood, although some bitches bleed more than others. They will also exude a smell advertising that they will soon be ready to mate. This smell is irresistible to male dogs and it is said that with a good wind a dog can smell a bitch in season six miles away!

Although she will attract many suitors, she will usually spurn their advances until between the tenth and fifteenth day, although care should be taken for the entire three weeks as these dates can vary from one bitch to another. Once this time arrives she will allow herself to be mated by any and every suitor, including her father, brothers or some from previous litters. Around sixty-three days later she will give birth to her puppies.

A bitch that escapes or is let out while in season is subjected to a most harrowing and unpleasant ordeal. After being pursued by any number of suitors, the most dominant and determined will fight for the right to mate with her, often inflicting terrible injuries on each other, and in many cases the bitch as well. If she is unwilling to mate she will be harassed and even attacked until she gives in. The pair will then join in what is known as a 'tie', usually for twenty to forty minutes (this can vary as well), although a tie is not essential for a successful mating. Then as soon as the two separate, a fight between the others ensues to see who will be next. Many bitches collapse from the exhaustion of constant matings, and from being chased non-stop for several days. This will go on continuously for two or three days, until her peak period is over. At this point the bitch can be severely injured by males who will not take no for an answer, and who may have had to wait several days for their turn. From start to finish a season normally lasts for three weeks, and occurs roughly every six months. How many of the owners who allow their bitches out when they are in season would swap places with her for even one day?

'Should I spay my bitch before or after her first season?'

Vet's opinions tend to vary on this question. Some say that, if you spay a bitch before her first season, although you can then forget the headache of keeping dogs away for weeks, this bitch may become incontinent when still fairly young. Some vets also feel that if you spay a bitch too young it will inhibit her proper development, as you will be spaying her before she has matured properly. The general recommendation is to let her have one season, taking care to ensure that she does not get mated. She can then be spayed midway between her seasons.

If you are doing this, when she is having the first season do not:

- Leave her unattended in the garden (male dogs can scale amazing heights with enough encouragement!).
- Let her off her lead during walks (you can use an extending lead to give more freedom).
- Assume that she will not mate with 'relatives'!
- Hope that just shutting the door on a male dog in the same house will stop him. Many a door has had to be replaced! If you have a male dog also it may be kinder

to find a friend or relative who will look after him for the duration of her season, depending upon how your dog copes with being in the same house as the bitch while she is on heat.

'If I castrate my dog, won't other dogs keep mounting him, thinking he is a bitch?'

This can happen yes. Male dogs give out a distinctive scent that is usually unmistakable to other males. But sometimes when they have been castrated the change in their scent confuses other dogs, and so they may decide to try their luck! But in most cases these seem to be the type of dog that will mount anything anyway, and a slight change in scent is as good excuse to try their luck as any other.

In summary, there are many reasons why you should neuter your dog or bitch, but no good reasons why you should not.

7   Identification

All dogs must by law (The Control of Dogs Order, 1992) wear a collar with the owner's details carried on it in some way whenever they are out in public. However, there are several other types of identification your dog can have. They are listed below, with advantages and disadvantages.

Collar and tag

This is the quickest and simplest way to contact an owner should the dog be found, and many more would be returned

to their owners much more quickly if they were wearing one. Without one, a great deal more effort is needed on the part of the finder, which is unfair and should not be necessary. Tags do get lost, so it is a good idea to get several cut so you always have a replacement to hand. A great many dogs that go missing do so from their own homes, but it is amazing how many owners take their dog's collar off when they are indoors. The result is that the dog escapes wearing no identification. Try to ensure that your dog wears its collar all the time.

Tattooing

This is commonly used on racing greyhounds, although it is gradually becoming more popular with pet owners. It stamps a permanent registration number, usually in the dog's ear, and so makes the dog traceable. In the event of theft, ownership is easily proven. The disadvantages are that sometimes the numbers are unreadable, which means that it has to be redone, and although it is over in a couple of seconds, it is very painful. Also, as there is more than one register it is difficult to know which one to contact. There are some breeds that must be tattooed by law, namely the breeds mentioned in the Dangerous Dogs Act such as the American Pit Bull Terrier and the Japanese Tosa.

Microchipping

This is the latest form of ID. It involves the injection of a microchip (about the size of a grain of rice) into the scruff of the neck. The chip will contain a number specific to you as the registered owner. It can be read by a special scanner. A lot of vets, the RSPCA, Battersea Dogs Home and other organisations all have scanners, so on finding a dog with a chip the owner's identity can very quickly be established. Having a chip is also a permanent form of owner identification in cases where pets have been stolen, and can eliminate lengthy battles over ownership.

8 Communication (What I Tell Him – What He Hears)

There are definite similarities in the way dogs and humans communicate. Both use vocalizations, facial expressions and gestures to convey our intentions, thoughts and feelings. Each group has also developed methods of making the other recognize some of those outward signals. It is a mistake, however, to assume that, because of those similarities in methods of communication, dogs 'understand' our language. They can, for example, learn to associate a particular sound with a particular action. If you ask a dog if it is hungry just before you feed it every day, it will not be long before the dog learns to associate the sound of this sentence with food, and will become excited when he hears it. However, the thing to remember in this case is that the dog *does not* understand the words that were spoken – only the tone. If you were to repeat the same sentence in a completely different tone with different inflections on the words, the dog would no longer recognize the question.

I frequently hear owners say their dogs 'understand every word' they say. What has usually happened is that the dog has learnt a sequence of events, and can predict the next stage. For example, many owners will say that their dog understands the commands 'IN THE CAR', and 'OUT OF THE CAR'. But what

I think that the dog has really learnt is the sequence. Through repetition he has realized that when he is taken to the car, the car door is opened and the owner says that familiar-sounding phrase, he is expected to get in the car. Similarly, when the car stops and the owner walks round to the back and opens the door and says the other familiar phrase, he is supposed to jump out of the car. This does not mean that the dog understands the words. If the owner were to walk the dog to the car and open the door and command the dog to get *out* of the car in the same tone as they would usually ask the dog to get into the car, chances are that the dog would jump in.

Case History – Don't you understand English, dog?

I was at a client's house, and her dog was being a bit of a nuisance, constantly demanding attention, jumping up and pawing to be stroked. She told the dog to go and lie down in its bed. The dog obeyed. Two minutes later it was back, misbehaving as before. So it was sent to bed again. This time it wasn't gone one minute before it was back. The owner snapped. 'If you don't go to your bed and stay there till I tell you to come out, you're really going to be in trouble.'

The dog ran back to his bed as he could tell that the owner was annoyed that he had reappeared, but because he had no idea what she had actually said, he failed to understand the threat of what would happen if he disobeyed again. As soon as he appeared the owner shot up and ran after him, shouting, 'That's it, don't say I didn't warn you!'

The problem here was that the owner had forgotten that at the end of the day she was talking to a dog. Because she had a very close, all-too-human relationship with him, she had attributed him with an understanding of our very complex language. What the dog probably heard was a system of growls, which clearly emphasized that the owner was angry, but nothing else that he could understand. In a situation like this one, the owner often gets very upset and punishes the dog as she feels that he is being deliberately disobedient. In fact, it is the owner who has failed the dog – she has obviously not properly taught him to understand what 'STAY' means, and she has failed to recognize his mental limitations. So who was really at fault: the dog or the owner?

Another example of us saying one thing and our dogs hearing another is when we use the command 'LEAVE'. When we tell our dog to leave something what we mean is don't approach or attempt to touch that object, as I have said that you cannot. What I think that some dogs actually hear is the owner saying I feel that this thing is very important so I want it all for myself. The result is that as soon as an owner says leave, the dog becomes desperate to get the object, feeling that it must be something very special, whereas if the owner had said nothing, the dog may have been much less interested in it.

There are two tests you can try on your dog to see how it views the 'LEAVE' command. Pick up two objects, neither should be food but both should be things that the dog is not very familiar with. Drop the first one on the floor near the dog, and for thirty seconds use your voice to encourage your dog to investigate it. Then drop the second object in a different spot, and use your voice to tell the dog not to touch it or to in any way investigate it. What some people find is that as soon as they tell the dog they can have the first object, the dog assumes that if he is being offered it, it can't be very valuable, and shows very little interest, regardless of how much the owner encourages him. But when he is told that he cannot have the second object, the dog assumes that it must be something very special, as most of the things that it is told it can't have are things that it really wants and it assumes you really want too. So he will try much harder to get them as soon as you tell him not to.

If your dog refuses to leave an object, you need to empower yourself in some way so that the dog takes the command seriously. It may simply be a case of raising your voice a little. If this doesn't work, try using a sound deterrent (described on p.177). This should shock him into obeying. You should then practise getting your dog to leave lots of different things in different environments, taking the deterrent with you if necessary. Remember though, that if your dog does leave something when told, you should reward that behaviour, bearing in mind that something is only a reward if the dog wants it at that time.

We see another example of this breakdown in communication in the park. Many owners take their dogs to a park purely so that the dog can do his own thing, running off to play with other dogs, explore new smells and generally pretty much forget that he is not out on his own, apart from the odd glance to make sure that his 'pet person' is still obediently following along behind him. The owners of these dogs seldom if ever attempt to interact with or entertain the dog themselves, they are simply the means by which the dog gets to and from the park. When they have finished walking the dog and are ready to go home, there is a monumental communication breakdown. The owner shouts 'Bonzo!', and means: 'Let's go home so that I can get ready for work, and earn the money to keep you in the style to which you have become accustomed.'

However, what Bonzo hears is: 'Fun time's over. Come here and let me put your lead on and take you back to the place where all of the control is exerted and there is much less of this kind of exciting stimulation.' Funnily enough, old Bonzo doesn't seem too keen to let the owner get within grabbing distance, and continually dances just out of reach infuriating Daddy, who can't understand why the dog does this twice a day every day.

Parents often repeat requests to their children several times without getting the desired response.

'Go upstairs and do your homework.'

'Oh, I really wanted to watch this.'

'You can watch it when you finish your homework.'

No response.

'Go and do your homework please.' (Slightly raised voice).

'Muuummmm.'

'WILL YOU GET UPSTAIRS AND DO YOUR HOMEWORK NOW!'

Suddenly there is a smell of burning carpet, and skid marks in the hall as the child races up the stairs. But what this child has learnt is that unless you shout at her, she may get away with not doing as she is told.

You see a very similar behaviour with dogs. Owners will ask the dog to do something two or three times, then tell it to do it another couple of times, then threaten it a couple more times, then punish it for not obeying in the first place. Each time the owner told the dog to do the task, the dog responded by saying, 'What happens if I refuse?' The owner repeats the command. The dog then learns that the only consequence of refusing is that it will be asked again. So it refuses again, and gets commanded again. But what the owner hasn't realized is that each time they repeat the command, they *reduce* the likelihood of the dog obeying that command, rather than increase it, as they are actually teaching the dog to ignore them.

So to summarize: keep commands brief. The longer the command, the harder it will be for the dog to learn. Having decided on a command, make sure that is the only command that is given in that context. For example, if you teach the dog that when you say 'DOWN' that it should lie down, don't then confuse the dog by sometimes saying 'LIE DOWN', and don't drone on with hopelessly long sentences that the dog cannot possibly follow.

9 Crime and Punishment

What is the best way to punish a dog? A rolled-up newspaper? A smack across the muzzle? Shutting him in another room, or in the garden? All of these are commonly used forms of punishment, but do they teach the dog the *correct* behaviour? Perhaps they make the situation worse, and can even teach other undesirable behaviour.

Does the dog recognize them as punishment for a crime it has committed? It is easy to punish a dog for doing something wrong, but unless the dog knows an alternative behaviour, it is quite likely to do it again.

For example, if you punish your dog for fouling indoors, without helping it learn to relieve itself outdoors, it will still foul indoors. All that will happen is that the dog will just get better at fouling at times when you are not there to catch it. So not only have you failed to cure the behaviour, you will have succeeded in making him much better at it and getting away with it too!

If your dog is destructive when you leave it, and when you come home hours later you punish him, next time you leave him he will probably be even more stressed because he now associates your going away with punishment. He does *not* know it is the destruction that he is being punished for, regardless of how guilty he looks. And of course the more stressed he is, the more likely he will be to want to vent that stress out on something, so he will be even more destructive. By punishing him you will probably only succeed in making him 'hand shy', so that he flinches every time you move your hand. Again you will have taught him undesirable behaviour without achieving anything positive.

Always use an appropriate punishment. For example, many people lock their dog out in the garden as a form of punishment. The theory is that the dog will have time to think about what it has done, and a little isolation may make it think twice about doing it again. This rarely works, as illustrated in the following case history.

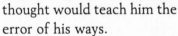

Case History – 'Hey Dad, can I have some isolation, please?'

A man rang me in total despair. He had a Jack Russell puppy that was *very* destructive. To punish the dog, the owner decided that he would put him outside in the garden. This he  thought would teach him the error of his ways.

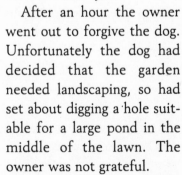

After an hour the owner went out to forgive the dog. Unfortunately the dog had decided that the garden needed landscaping, so had set about digging a hole suitable for a large pond in the middle of the lawn. The owner was not grateful.

After some serious cursing from the owner, the dog was brought indoors for isolation number two: the bathroom. The dog had never been allowed upstairs, so the owner thought that leaving the dog in an unfamiliar room was bound to distress him. Wrong! After a while, the owner went up to see how the dog was repenting. He found the dog had decided that the bathroom colour scheme was all wrong, and so had set about stripping the wallpaper.

The mistake that the owner made was that he was trying to use a punishment that the dog saw as a reward. Inevitably, it failed to teach the dog the lesson that the owner had wanted it to learn.

You must also be careful always to let the punishment fit the crime. If you give your puppy old shoes to play with, then one day he destroys your favourite pair of expensive leather shoes, do not be quick to blame him, after all who was it that gave him shoes to chew in the first place? How is he supposed to know the difference between an old shoe and a new one, or between a cheap and expensive pair?

A better idea is to try to think ahead so that you do not leave the dog in a situation that is likely to cause a problem to either of you. For instance, if you have a dog that chews, leave him something to occupy him, but remember things that he has constant access to will not be as interesting as things that he doesn't. So if you leave him an interesting toy, do not leave toys scattered all around the house all of the time. Reserve one or two for times when you are not able to supervise him, so that those toys keep their novelty, and pick them up again immediately on your return. Do not leave easily destructible toys because he may chew them into pieces and become ill if he swallows them.

If you do have to punish the dog, the type of punishment that you use and how much will depend upon what it is the dog has done, the age of the dog, and your relationship with it. For example, a very young puppy can for a *serious* misbe-haviour be sternly shaken by the scruff, the loose skin on the back of the neck. If done correctly, the puppy should yelp the way it would if it's mother had done it. This is a punishment that dogs use on other dogs, so they recognize it and what it means. However, it is this very fact that prevents it being used on other types of dog. If you tried to use it on a fully grown dog that was already showing aggression towards its owners, the consequences could be severe. The dog would instantly recognize this as a humiliating form of punishment, and may not accept the owner trying to use it.

Case History – A Little knowledge is a dangerous thing

A mother rang me for advice. She owned a 6-year-old male Labrador/Rottweiler cross. She also had a 5-year-old boy. The dog had never been keen on the boy, and the mother had always had to keep a close eye on the dog, as she did not fully trust him around the child. The child had therefore been taught to give the dog a wide berth. Recently however, the dog had started to growl at the boy just for moving, even if it was not in the dog's direction. The mother had tried telling the dog off, but the situation was nonetheless getting worse. So in desperation, she rang her vet. He advised her that the dog needed to learn to respect the child. He said that there was no point in her punishing the dog, the boy would have to do it.

Astonishingly, he recommended that the child should grab the dog by the scruff of its neck and shake it as hard as he could. This, he said, would teach the dog to respect the child as being higher ranked than he was. The mother decided that she would give it a go, and was explaining to her son what to do when the doorbell rang. It was a woman who happened to know me through some work that I had done with her and her dog. She advised the mother to ring me before doing this, as she knew my view on confrontational battles with adult dogs.

I firmly believe that if the child had tried to do this, the dog would have at best bitten him badly. I don't like to think what would have happened at worst, but we are talking about a 5-year-old boy against a dog that was almost as tall as him, and probably weighed three times as much, with a set of jaws able to exert perhaps as much as 200 pounds per square inch. I decided that I would contact the vet to discuss the matter, as I felt that this advice had been potentially very dangerous.

So if the dog is older, and is using any form of aggression towards you, try using a form of punishment that means you don't have to have a fight. A soft drink can with pebbles in it thrown in the dog's direction without it hitting the dog can shock it into stopping a behaviour. Or the use of other loud noises such as a panic alarm can provide a temporary break in whatever the dog is doing. (Sound deterrents are discussed in full on p.177.) Sometimes a water pistol can have the same effect, though dogs can quickly become de-sensitized to them. If you have a sensitive dog, you may find that verbal chastisement is sufficient, in which case there is no need to use anything else.

Many people think that if a dog fouls indoors, the correct form of punishment is to rub the dog's nose in it. Apart from the danger of leaving deposits of faeces up the dog's nostrils, which the dog may not be able to get out, this seems to increase the likelihood of the dog becoming coprophagic (eating its own faeces). This is a good way for the owner to ensure that the dog gets lots of opportunities to acquire a taste for it by forcing him to have to lick it off his face.

Try always to reward correct behaviour rather than focusing on punishing the wrong behaviour. That way the dog will learn what is wanted of it much quicker, rather than learning what is wrong without actually being shown an alternative. And always ensure that the punishment fits the crime.

10 Obedience Training: The Modern Approach

The way in which dogs are trained has changed dramatically since the seventies and eighties, when dog training relied upon a high level of punishment in order to achieve any level of success. What these methods overlook is the fact that training this way carries a price. The dog, like a person in the same situation, cannot be relied upon to do a job well, if it resents the work that it is doing because it is unrewarding. Nowadays, much more emphasis is placed upon ensuring that the dog enjoys the work that it is being asked to do, and that it is rewarded for doing it, so that it wants to do it again.

Toilet training

Most puppies are toilet trained when they leave their mothers. It is we who teach them to foul indoors. When the puppy was with his mother he would wake up, leave the 'nest', relieve himself and then go and have a feed. Then, when he had finished eating he might relieve himself again, have a play, have one last attempt and then go back to sleep. But for all those trips to the toilet he would leave the place where he slept and go where it was acceptable to empty.

Where owners sometimes go wrong is that they fail to realize how often a puppy needs to relieve itself and so they leave it no alternative but to foul in the house. Then they punish it for not being clean. Try to bear in mind that human babies take far longer to dispense with nappies and use the toilet than puppies take to learn to use the garden. But if a child messed in his or her nappy or wet the bed would you rub his or her nose in it? People often do this with puppies, thinking it will make them clean. Stop and think how absurd that is! It is generally accepted that seconds after a puppy has fouled it will have forgotten that it did it, so to punish it minutes, even hours later is absolutely pointless. Although he may recognize that the faeces has his scent, he will not remember how the faeces got there, so rubbing his nose in it will teach him absolutely nothing useful.

So in the home environment we must try to give the puppy every opportunity to get it right. Most people put down newspaper and try to get the puppy used to relieving itself on it. This is fine, providing that you do not expect the pup to just magically cotton on and start using the garden or the park. Unless you follow through with additional training, all that usually happens is that the puppy learns that it is supposed to empty at home on the newspaper. So the pup will go for an entire walk, but will wait to get home so that he can relieve himself in the place where he has been taught! One day he comes home to find no newspaper, because you have decided that it is about time he started doing it outside. But chances are that he will now do it in the place where the newspaper used to be, or he may become confused and just do it anywhere in the house.

The times that your puppy will be most likely to want to

relieve itself will be when he wakes up, after he has had a period of excitement (such as a bout of play), and after meals. He may also need to go in between these times as well. Armed with this knowledge, we can start to train our puppy to relieve itself on command.

Pick a word or phrase that will come to mean relieve yourself now, such as 'BE CLEAN'. Take the puppy into the garden and wait, standing quite close to it. As soon as the puppy begins to relieve himself, use your new command a few times, also telling him what a good dog he is. As soon as he is finished go to him and make a *huge* fuss of him. It is important that you go to the dog, rather than call the dog to you, as if you do call the dog and then reward him, he will think that he is being rewarded for coming to you, and not for being clean. After you have repeated this exercise for a while, the puppy will hear the command to empty himself and will immediately try to do so. *Every* time he goes where you want him to, make a big fuss of him. Now he should have got the idea of where it is best to relieve himself. If you catch him in the act, and *only* if you catch him *in the act* of fouling anywhere, use a short word such as 'NO', pick him up and quickly put him outside to finish relieving himself. When he does so give him lots of praise as usual for the correct behaviour.

There is a method you can try using that involves newspaper, but make sure that no one is reading it at the time! Put down plenty of paper at first so it is difficult for him to miss it, rewarding him every time he gets it right. Once he is reliably using it, gradually, over a period of a week or two, reduce the amount of paper to one sheet. Then, again over a period of days, gradually move the paper towards the garden door. Once he will relieve himself there, start to put the paper outside the door and take him to it every two or three hours, encouraging him to go to the toilet (this will reduce the chance of an 'accident' indoors). If he does go, make a *huge* fuss of him. When he is reliably going on the newspaper move it to a spot in the garden where you are happy for him to go. When he is reliably going to the correct place start gradually to reduce the size of the paper until there is only a tiny piece left. After a few days you can remove that piece too. He should now, after a short search for his piece of paper, mess in the place he is used to.

Even if your puppy is older and still fouling indoors this can still be cured, but it is obviously a little more difficult as now the puppy has got into a bad habit. Sometimes they do this because, as already discussed, they now believe that they are *supposed* to foul indoors. Maybe they are scent-marking their territory in many places around the house, often the case of maturing male dogs. Male dogs can urinate in the house for several different reasons. Sometimes, they are simply 'marking their territory', other times it can be due to a sense of insecurity. Some dogs can even use this in an effort to assert their dominance over an owner. Or he might just have a bladder problem.

But let us assume that because of the wrong training the dog now goes out for a long walk every day and then comes home and fouls in the house. Let us imagine that every day you take him for an hour's walk, and that after ten minutes of that walk your dog is absolutely bursting to go to the toilet. So what you do now is, instead of walking for another fifty minutes, you take him home. When you get there he will want to go straight in to relieve himself, but do not let him in. Instead, take him out to the back garden or back to the park. The chances are he will have psyched himself up to go so much that he will probably do it straight away. You can then praise him, and if you keep this up he should get the idea.

Some dogs seem to mess in the house as though they just

cannot be bothered to wait a short while until you return. If this is the case, try putting him in an indoor kennel for the short periods that he will be left unsupervised (you can usually borrow or buy 'collapsible' kennels). Most dogs will not foul the area in which they sleep. As soon as you return, let him out to relieve himself and give him lots of praise as usual.

In all of this training the large amount of praise that you give when they get it right is very important. If this reward is not given the dog will not know he has got it right, and so is less likely to realize that he is meant to do that again.

The training class

For everything that you attempt to teach your dog, be it at home or at obedience classes, there will be a number of different approaches. The difficult part is to decide which one will work best for you and your dog. If you are thinking of joining an obedience class, it is a good idea to go along as soon as possible after your puppy has had his vaccinations. He needs as much socializing as he can get, and leaving him alone until he is six months old will result in a lot of problems that may by then be much more difficult to put right.

However, no instructor always gets it right, sometimes through no fault of their own. Perhaps the owner has missed telling them something that would have affected the instructor's behaviour, or it can be that a particular dog does not respond to a certain type of training. Sometimes the action that the instructor chooses does not work, not because of the instructor or the method recommended, but because the owner doesn't teach the exercise the way in which the instructor advised them to.

Most instructors will probably have played a part in training several hundred dogs over the years and so should have a fairly good idea of what works and what doesn't. Compare that to how many dogs that you personally have trained. If you feel the need to train differently from how you are instructed, speak to the trainer, as he may agree that your suggestion is better. If he does not, he should be able to give you the reasons why. If you are still not happy, maybe you should change to a different obedience class. But what you shouldn't do is work the instructor's way at your class, and your own way everywhere else. This will only confuse the dog. Neither should you simply give up training the dog. Sadly he is not likely to one day suddenly wake up cured of his problems.

Sometimes, a training class can teach your dog something that you really didn't want him to learn.

Case History – He who barks last, barks longest

A young woman enrolled at my class with a Border Collie. The dog was very excitable, but basically had a sound temperament. He was good with both people and other dogs. Also enrolled on the course was a woman with a German Shepherd. On enrolment night, I ask everyone if their dogs are good with other dogs, as if they are not, they may need dealing with as a behavioural client, rather than in a training class. Everyone said that their dogs were fine.

When this Shepherd came through the door however, it was clearly anything but fine. It launched itself at the nearest dog, barking furiously. I advised the owner that we would have to pull the dog from the class if this continued, but the owner insisted that the dog would settle down in a while.

For some reason, this Shepherd took an instant dislike to

the Border Collie. Perhaps it was because he was only young and never retaliated, so she felt more comfortable about having a go at a seemingly defenceless victim. But after a while, he started to notice this dog, even though both owners tried to keep them as far apart as possible.

By week three of the course, the collie had had enough, and had started barking back, much to the fury of the Shepherd, who now went berserk every time that they laid eyes on each other or if the collie so much as moved.

By the end of the course, not only did the collie despise the Shepherd, but he had decided that he disliked *all* Shepherds, and had gone for any German Shepherd that he met while out on walks. So the class environment had been at least partly responsible for teaching this dog to hate other dogs. In a less confined area such as the local park, this would probably never have happened, but in the small area of a church hall, where the dogs have less opportunity to avoid each other, tempers can easily flare. With additional training, both owners were able to deal with their dogs' aggression. Although the German Shepherd was never completely reliable, the Border Collie was fine after a little extra training.

When it comes to enrolling at a class, you will find that different classes have different payment schemes. The more traditional class tends to have a yearly subscription, and then a small sum that is paid every time that the owner actually turns up at class. In this class, you can attend for anything from a few years to the day the dog dies of old age.

The advantage in this method is that people tend to stay for a long time, often well after their initial problem has been cured. The instructor often develops close relationships with some of the members, who come to regard the class as a social evening, and never work very hard with their dogs. However, this can also be a disadvantage. I remember an incident that occurred when I used to run my club this way. A very nice lady used to come to the class with a Jack Russell. He was only very young, but very excitable and boisterous, and his owner sensibly decided to train him before he became too much for her.

The dog responded well, and she soon got him to the point where he did everything that she wanted. One day, after attending classes regularly for several months, she turned up without him.

'What's wrong with the dog?' I asked.

'Nothing,' she replied.

'Well, where is he?' I enquired.

The owner looked down and gasped. 'Would you believe it?' she said. 'As I left the house I knew I had forgotten something!'

This illustrates how this social evening attitude can get in the way of genuine training. She forgot her dog because that was no longer her main reason for coming. While that is very flattering for me, it is not why I am here.

The disadvantage of running a class this way is that because people are reluctant to leave, it is often very difficult to enrol new people, as the class is filled with people who really shouldn't be there. They have already cured their dogs, but don't want to leave. It can also be detrimental to the dogs, as some of them will develop relationships with other dogs that may not always be pleasant ones. For example, if you get two dogs in the hall that do not get on after one week, what might they be like after one year? This method also means that people can join the class at any time, so the members who have been there for a while are constantly having to wait while new members are taught the basics, things that the rest of the class may have learnt months or even years ago.

The more progressive classes tend to run courses that last for a pre-stated number of weeks. Owners are charged a course fee, which is usually paid before, or at the first lesson. Under this method, owners often work harder, as they have already paid for the course, and want to get their money's worth. This also means that the drop-off rate is lower, as again, because people have already paid for it, they are much more likely to see it through. In addition, the pupils are at the same stage, so they are less likely to join feeling as though they are holding the rest of the class up.

Choosing a training class:

Choosing the right training class is something that you should spend some time doing, as joining the wrong one can have disastrous effects on your dog and your relationship with him.

Case History – Why leave the club with just one problem?

This is a story that was told to me by a colleague. A man went to a dog training class with his 18-month-old Labrador cross. The only problem that the dog had was that it pulled on the lead. The instructor came from a services background, and was quite a disciplinarian. The owner was ordered to get the dog under control. When he failed, the instructor took the dog from the owner, put a check chain on the dog and walked it around the hall several times, checking it severely every few feet, telling the owner that what the dog needed was to learn respect. After a few minutes of this, the dog seemed very stressed, but was walking a lot better, so it was handed back to the owner. As the owner went to take the lead, the dog jumped gratefully towards him. The instructor yanked the dog back, saying that he'd have none of that jumping up lark either. The owner tried again. This time the dog kept all four feet on the ground. For the next few circuits of the hall, the dog kept a wary eye on the instructor, who also kept a close eye on him.

The following week the owner arrived at the class and was surprised to see his dog rush aggressively at the nearest dog to him as soon as they entered the hall. The instructor rushed over and grabbed the lead. The owner explained that he had never seen the dog be aggressive towards another dog before, he was normally absolutely friendly with everything. 'Well, we'll soon stop that getting out of hand,' replied the instructor, and the dog was subjected to more checking.

Over the next couple of weeks, the dog's behaviour towards other dogs worsened, and he even began to growl at certain people that approached him, especially men. The owner felt more and more unhappy with his dog's sudden aggressive behaviour. At the class, he was often quieter than outside, and if he ever did bark, the instructor was always quick to get hold of him.

One day a new dog arrived at the hall, and as soon as it came through the door, our Labrador cross flew at it. As the instructor went to grab the lead, the dog jumped up and bit him in the place where all men would probably least want to be bitten. The instructor had to be taken to hospital, and the wound required stitching. The dog's owner was told that he would no longer be welcome at the class, as his dog was too aggressive, and really ought to be put to sleep.

This is a good example of a case where it was actually the class itself and the way that the instructor ran it that brought the dog owner to a point where he was considering putting his dog to sleep for its aggression. When he joined the class, the dog had a superb temperament, and its only vice was that it pulled on the lead.

When looking at classes, there are several things you can do to help you make the right choice.

- Try to look at as many different clubs as you can before or soon after you get your puppy. This should mean that you can join *before* he becomes too much of a problem!
- Different trainers use different methods so look at as many as possible to see which suits you best.
- Price is no indication of quality when it comes to obedience classes, so do not join the most expensive hoping to get the best.
- Look for a class where you are not packed in like sardines! Obviously if there are too many people and dogs in a hall this will limit the amount of individual help you can expect to receive. It will also place a lot more pressure on both you and your dog, as you will always be too close to the dog next to you.
- Try to find a class that teaches the type of things you need to learn. Lots of classes try to teach beginner dogs and handlers exercises that are geared towards competition obedience, and this may not be what you are looking for.
- Look at the way the instructor deals with the people that are already members. Look for members who are clearly having problems with their dog and watch how the instructor deals with them. The instructor should keep offering to help them. But if you see the instructor ignoring that person or pretending they do not see them in distress, it should give you a fair idea of what will happen to you should you hit problems.
- Check for the instructor who simply 'herds' his members around the room! That is to say, he tells them when to stop, go, turn and so on, but gives them no encourage-

ment or correction if they get a part of an exercise wrong. He just moves them along and then goes on to the next one. How much are his members likely to improve.

- Try to find a class where there is a friendly atmosphere and where people are willing to offer you advice without you feeling uncomfortable about asking, and where the instructor seems genuinely interested in helping you. However, also bear in mind most instructors will probably have at least one member who, regardless of what they say or advise, simply will not do as they are asked, and never practise outside the class. These people are usually easy for the instructor to spot in a class situation, and so in time some trainers may decide to stop wasting time with this person and devote that time to those who really want to improve.

These are some of the things that you will need to be vigilant about when choosing a class. It is a good idea to leave your dog at home on the nights you go to look at classes so you will not be distracted by him. All classes should be happy for you to go along and watch. But remember, whichever class you join, you will only get out the amount of work that you put in. If you only practise once a week at the club, you are unlikely to make a significant improvement.

Below are some of the exercises that you may be taught at an obedience class, and some of the more common mistakes owners make when trying both to learn themselves, and to teach their dogs.

Heelwork

This is where the dog walks beside you without pulling. Teaching this can be a lot more difficult than it sounds.

In the more traditional dog training class, owners will usually be expected to fit their dog with a check chain. Sometimes the owner will be instructed to get one even if the dog doesn't pull on the lead. The class will form a circle around the perimeter of the hall. They then all commence walking in the same direction, clockwise or anti-clockwise. The owners will be instructed to yank or check the lead every time that the dog pulls them, telling the dog to heel. Periodically the owners will be told to about-turn and go around in the opposite direction. They will also be told to halt, at which point the whole class should stop walking and place their dogs in a sit. There is often less emphasis on rewards in this type of class, certainly less food or toy rewards. They are restricted to verbal or physical rewards whether they are what the dog wants or not.

The advantage for the instructor in using this method of heelwork is that you can fit a lot of dogs into a relatively small area, which means more pupils.

The disadvantage with this method is that it actually *encourages* dogs to pull on the lead, as they either want to catch up to the dog in front of them, or they want to get away from the dog that is coming up behind them. The result is that owners find the class very stressful, as the dog seems worse there than anywhere else, which often damages the owner's confidence. Having more dogs in the hall also means that each individual owner finds it harder to avoid the other dogs. All you need is one person travelling slower than the others, and you soon end up with a traffic jam!

In the more progressive class, the dogs tend to be worked in much smaller groups. The heelwork is done in groups, walking parallel in a line across the hall, or in informal zigzags with no set route at all, so dogs pass each other at any moment. This reduces the dogs pulling, as they are not so close to the other dogs. Much more emphasis is placed on rewards in this type of class, and many more types of reward are used.

For some owners, a head collar or a body harness can be helpful, though they only prevent the dog from pulling rather than actually teaching it not to. You can often wean the dog from one of these aids by taking it off for short periods when the dog is walking well, and replacing it the second the dog begins to pull again. Hopefully the dog will learn that it is in his best interest not to pull.

Some dogs respond well to owners who suddenly change direction, checking the dog firmly after them, whenever it pulls on the lead, though this can mean that it takes a lot longer to get where you want to go.

Many dog owners also have a real misunderstanding of the way that a check chain is supposed to work. Contrary to what seems to be popular belief, you do not simply put it on and let the dog choke himself until he decides that it is too painful and stops pulling. Those of you who have tried that no doubt now have a dog that pulls until he near-collapses from choking, then gets up and starts pulling again. To use a check chain correctly you must firstly ensure that it is put on the correct way. Putting it on upside down is quite dangerous for the dog. When correctly fitted with the chain, the dog has to stay on the same side of you as he was on when you put the chain on him, otherwise it will then be upside down.

Assuming that the chain is now on the correct way, it should then be firmly checked every time that the dog moves even one pace in front of you, long before he is pulling on the lead. That way, he is supposed to learn to stay where he is.

Personally, I do not like check chains, as I do not feel that they are really necessary, except in a very few cases, and even then, only with someone who knows how to use one correctly. One of the most common mistakes with this type of training is that the owner walks along jerking the lead almost constantly, never hard enough for the dog to actually respond to it as a correction, as it should, but just hard enough to keep pulling the dog's head. What is the purpose of this? It merely nags continually at the dog without you really teaching it anything at all. Another common mistake is to check or pull the lead to get the dog's attention before you even start walking, before the dog has actually done anything wrong, and sometimes even before you have said his name. Many people do not even say the dog's name at all when they are doing heelwork, relying on some 'psychic bond' they share to let him know that they are going to walk off. Instead, they just march off – if the dog wasn't paying attention, he gets a yank on the lead.

Be careful not to allow the dog to pull you to places like the park because it is easier to let them than to correct them. Lots of people make it harder for themselves and their dog by working their dog with a treat or toy at the club, but never using one at home or in the park when training. What the dog is probably learning is that work is only enjoyable at classes. Many people spend an hour or so on club night teaching the dog to stop pulling, and then, when the class is over, let the dog *drag* them out of the door, down the street to the car! This again teaches the dog that it only has to walk to heel at the class.

There are a great number who tell the dog to sit as many as four or five times to see if he will. What you should do is put him into the sit on the *first* command until he always does it straight away, otherwise he is simply being taught to ignore you when you tell him to do something. Always try to encourage the dog. Try not to plod around, giving no indication to the dog of the difference between right and wrong, again relying on the good old 'psychic bond' to tell the dog what is correct. You do not necessarily have to start your heelwork session with a sit (although you will usually be asked to at dog clubs), but if you do remember the above.

Be careful not to give too little praise because you are embarrassed in front of strangers. Because of this embarrassment, owners are often too quick to administer punishment when the dog does something wrong because they feel he has made them look silly. What is more likely to happen is that people will look at you and think how hard you are because you never praise your dog, but are always shouting at him and jerking on the check chain. Remember you may think that people will laugh at you, but in reality, they will probably be far too busy with their own dogs. If you neglect a part of your dog's training because you are too self-conscious, who will lose out, those 'laughing', or you and your dog?

Recall

This exercise should teach the dog to come back when called. As with heelwork, this exercise should be enjoyable for dog and owner. For most people, the place your dog is least likely to come back when called is the park. Why is this?

Imagine this scenario. You are a young puppy that has just been taken out for his first walk after his vaccinations. With luck, your owner will have been carrying you on walks prior to vaccinations, so you are already very keen to play with the dogs you have seen, especially as you really miss your litter mates. They take you to the park, but because they are worried that you may not come back, they do not let you off the lead. Now you are even more frustrated because the other dogs come up and sniff you then run away, but when you try to chase them the lead pulls you back. This goes on for several weeks/months, with the owner believing that if you are not let off the lead you will learn to stay with them.

Finally the big day comes and the lead is removed. At first you only move a short distance away and the owner is pleased. Then another dog comes over to you. You give a few tentative squeals because it is very big compared to you, and a bit rough, but soon you realize there is no danger. Then the other dog's owner calls him and off he goes. Not wishing to lose your new-found friend you now chase after him and *wham*! Suddenly you realize that you can run and run and nothing is holding you back. Off you go, having a wonderful time, oblivious to everything except having fun. You hear your owner calling you in that angry voice that you have already learnt means you are in trouble, but you don't know why. So back you go to your owner, who picks you up, shouts and scolds you, using words that mean nothing to you like: 'You bad dog, it's very naughty to run off like that!'

If your pup is *very* clever, he may just pick out the words 'BAD DOG' from all of that, but will have no idea why he was bad. The next day, as he will now have completely forgotten what happened the day before, the puppy does exactly the same thing. This time you are even more cross when he eventually comes back, and you tell him off even more angrily than the day before. The third day when you take him out you decide he needs more time spent on the lead, but the puppy now has had a taste of freedom and cannot wait to run loose again.

Three months pass, and Puppy is just beginning to feel his first sexual stirrings. You take him to the park, and decide that maybe now he has learnt his lesson. You let him off the lead. Almost instantly, you see a dog on the other side of the park that looks just like yours. Come to think of it, where is yours? Now when you call him he takes no notice. He has already been taught that to come back means to be punished, but to not come back means you can have fun! Which would you choose?

How does all this help you? Make sure that you *always* have a reward for your dog when you recall it. Remember, everything your dog learns, it learns on a reward/punishment/no consequence basis. Try only to recall your dog when he is likely to obey. If you give him a command you know he will disobey because the other reward is greater than yours, do not give him the chance to ignore it. When he does return, however long it has taken him to do so, always reward him, though he shouldn't get the best reward if he didn't come immediately you called him. He should learn that it is profitable for him to do as he is told. Remember, the more your dog hears you call his name, and the more often when he gets to you he is well rewarded, the more likely he will be to do it again. You should practice this indoors as well as out. It is also a good idea to attach a consequence to not responding (see Chapter 9).

In the traditional class, the recall taught is basically a beginner competitive recall. That is to say, it is the type of recall that you would have to do in an obedience competition, and is completely unrelated to getting your dog to come back in the park. It normally has this format. The owner will place the dog in the sit position. They will tell the dog to wait, and leave the dog to the end of the lead and then turn and face it. When the instructor tells the owner to, and not before, they must call the dog to them. the dog must then run up to the owner and sit in front of them, as straight as possible. The dog then does another exercise called a finish, which involves the dog walking around the back of the owner and sitting on the owner's left-hand side.

Unfortunately, this exercise bears no resemblance to what the owner encounters when out walking their dog. When they go to call their dog in the park, he is never in the sit position in front of them at the end of the lead. He is running around chasing another dog or following a scent. So he fails to recognize this as the exercise that he did in training school, and so doesn't respond. The owner is able to do a novice recall standing fifty yards away from the dog, with him sitting while they face him. But they still can't get him to come back in the park.

In the modern class, recalls will involve calling the dog away from other dogs, from food, from people and toys. These exercises will usually be done on a slack lead, or with no lead at all, and usually with little or no control being placed on the dog prior to his being called, so he learns to respond without being put in a controlled environment before he starts.

Stay on command

This exercise teaches the dog to stay until he is given a release command by the owner. A dog will only reliably stay in a position away from the owner if he is confident that the owner will return.

In the traditional class, this exercise is usually taught in such a way that most of the dogs are almost bound to fail. The most common mistake made on stays is that the owner can't resist testing the dog to see if he has learnt to stay yet. Some owners, when told by the instructor at an obedience class to 'only go *one* pace away', will try to go three or four. And then as soon as the instructor turns to look at another dog, they go a couple more. When the dog gets worried, and gets up, they go back to it growling and snarling about what a bad dog it was. Now the dog is stressed and a little worried. The owner then marches off again, not learning from their previous mistake because they are thinking 'I know he can do this'. Because the dog is now worried, he gets up even sooner than last time. So now the owner is really annoyed, and drags him back by the scruff of his neck, and very firmly bares his teeth at the dog and warns him to stay. This time he is genuinely frightened, so before the owner can even get a foot away he gets up. The owner is just about to throttle the dog when the instructor comes over and asks how he is getting on. Not wishing to look as though things are getting worse instead of better, he replies that he is doing fine! But what has the dog really learnt? Probably that it is unpleasant to be left, so it is best to follow his owner, but if he follows he will be punished. Therefore this attitude most certainly won't make him reliable on a stay.

It is essential that the distance that you leave the dog is built up very gradually, a pace at a time to start with, so the dog is not put under too much pressure and is confident that you will come back for him.

The more modern trainer will try to ensure that the dog never gets the exercise wrong in the first place, eliminating the need for correction or punishment. So they never increase the distance until the dog is one hundred per cent reliable on the present distance – or all they will achieve is unreliable stays. They reward the dog all the time while it is doing the right thing, instead of standing there glaring at the dog, daring it not to move. And most importantly, they don't keep punishing the dog for moving, as all this means is that they have failed to teach the dog the exercise correctly.

Socializing

There will usually be some sort of socializing exercise to get dogs used to interacting with other dogs without trying to leap all over them, dragging the owner with them.

In the traditional class, this is often a 'weaving' exercise. You all sit your dogs in a circle around the perimeter of the hall. One at a time each owner weaves in and out of the others telling his dog to 'LEAVE' as he passes each one, while the other owners stand still telling their own dogs to leave yours. A common mistake with this exercise is that people again want to test the dog to see if he will leave the oncoming dog and handler, so they say nothing. Then when their dog jumps up barking at the approaching one, they punish it for disobeying, when in fact the dog was given no command in the first place! How can he disobey what he hasn't been asked to do?

In my opinion this is a terrible exercise. Firstly, it is not a socializing exercise at all, since the dogs are never allowed to meet, and are punished for trying. Secondly, it gives a lot of dogs a good chance to have a go at the dogs that they don't like and whose owners have spent the entire night trying to keep apart. You can almost see some dogs rolling their sleeves up as soon as that circle is formed, while others have to be dragged into that circle, as they know that they are about to be roared at. I do not know of a good socializing exercise that can be done in a class situation with dogs of all ages, breeds and sizes, nor have I seen one I would recommend in all the many classes I have visited.

Some other exercises taught at more progressive classes include stopping dogs jumping up, food refusal, physical examination of the dogs, and play exercises.

The ironic thing about the exercises that I have just criticized is that at some time, in some class, I myself have taught them all. Fortunately, I have come to see their shortcomings, and have tried to find ways to improve upon them, either by myself or by studying the work of others. What did it for me was one day looking through my club register and asking myself how many of the people who had left my club over the years had left because I had cured all of the problems with which they had come to me. It is something that I would recommend all instructors think about. Many people come to us as their last resort. Indeed, some dogs have been put to sleep as a direct result of going to the wrong training class. We owe it to these people, who have paid us to help them, to do the very best that we are able. If I ever get to a stage where I am not prepared to do that, then will be the time to call it a day.

In every aspect of his training, put yourself in the dog's position. Think well ahead and ask yourself if what you are planning to do makes sense, to you *and* your dog. Also ask yourself why the dog would think that it is to his advantage to do as you are asking him. If the only thing compelling him to do as he is told is a threat of punishment, the dog may well learn a way of doing what he likes and still avoid the punishment, thereby rewarding himself. Try not to focus too much on the things that the dog gets wrong in training. Instead, ask yourself if the dog fully understands what is required of it, or if the mistake is more down to the fact that you haven't taught the dog what it is that you want from him. Remember, you would do nothing for nothing. Why should your dog be treated any differently?

Recommended reading on this subject

Hunter, Roy, *Fun and Games with Dogs* (Howln Moon Press, Maine, 1993)

Rogerson, John, *Training Your Dog* (Popular Dogs Publishing, 1997)

Ryan, Terry, *The Toolbox for Remodelling Your Problem Dog* (Howell Book House, New York, 1998)

11 Dogs and the Law

There are several laws in this country relating to dogs. Most of them are not likely to affect the average dog owner. Some are bylaws created and enforced by a local authority. Others will relate to housing, and terms and conditions under which a dog can be kept, and again may have been introduced by a council or housing association. Then there are those that were introduced by the government. Here are some of the ones more likely to affect the average dog owner.

Straying dogs

There are many reasons why people allow their dog to stray. Perhaps they let him out while they are at work, to stop him wrecking the house out of boredom. Maybe he is not clean indoors when left, or it could be that he jumps the fence and escapes. At the end of the day all these reasons are preventable, and even dogs that have been doing these things for a very long time can usually be put right.

There are many owners who really cannot see anything wrong with allowing their dog to stray. The dog is not aggressive, all the neighbours know him and feed him, the children play with him – so what's the problem? Well to give an example of just such a problem, here is a true story of something that happened not long ago.

Case History – A High price for an owner's laziness

The local authority received a call about a man who let his German Shepherd stray down the street and around the corner to the green to relieve itself every day. The dog was let out in the daytime for all the reasons I described at the beginning of this paragraph, and so, in spite of warnings from the dog warden that the dog would be picked up, the owner continued to allow it to stray.

One day as the dog was turning the corner to go to the green, a small boy was turning the corner from the opposite direction. Because the boy was frightened of dogs, he jumped backwards, fell into the road and was hit by a car. He suffered a fractured collarbone and facial injuries, but it could obviously have been very much worse. If you are one of those people who allows their dog to stray, think carefully about the consequences. Who knows how many accidents your dog may have already caused?

Every year animal welfare organisations pick up injured stray dogs that have been involved in accidents. All too often owners who let their dogs stray are not in attendance when their own animal is injured, and it is left to the animal welfare organisations or well-meaning members of the public to deal with such incidents. Anyone injured as a result of a dog straying would have very good grounds to take legal action against the owner.

Dogs who have strayed all their lives may appear 'streetwise', but when older they are at far greater risk to both themselves and other road users. Their sight diminishes, as does their hearing, and as they become slower, they will not always be quick enough to avoid the car that a few years earlier would have missed them. 'He's never been in an accident before' is, amazingly, a statement made all too frequently by the owners of such animals, who often appear genuinely surprised that their pet has been run over – despite the fact that they know he crosses many roads each day.

Obviously if you are not with your dog you will have no control over where and when it relieves itself. But due to territorial scent marking, once a garden has been used by one dog, it will probably be used by many more. This is plainly unfair on the resident to whom the garden belongs, and can create a health hazard. It is much more sensible to ensure that not only do you take an active part in exercising your dog, but that you allow it to relieve itself in the appropriate places. This is especially important in places where children play, such as parks and play areas. If there are dog exercise areas, use them, as this lessens the chance that a child may play where a dog has fouled. Where possible, clean up after your dog using a 'poop scoop' or an airtight plastic bag.

If an un-castrated male dog is allowed to roam, chances are that when he reaches sexual maturity he will actively seek out bitches, especially ones that are in season. If the bitch concerned is out on the loose herself, he will, along with other males in the area, mate with her, and unwanted puppies are usually the result. Often male dogs will fight over a female, and if a bitch is repeatedly mated she can become exhausted and ill, not to mention badly injured. Even if a bitch is in her own garden, a straying male will go to enormous lengths to reach her!

So what are the consequences for people who still let their dog stray? Under the Animals Act 1971, owners or keepers have a 'duty to take reasonable care to see that injury or damage is not caused by their animals straying on to the road'. It is therefore illegal for a dog to be unattended in a public place. 'In public' literally means anywhere other than on the property of the dog's owner. This covers places such as roads, pavements, communal gardens/greens, balconies and any other place where the general public have access. Dogs straying can intimidate people who are frightened of them, especially the young and the elderly, both of whom are at greater risk of falling over and injuring themselves trying to get away from a stray dog. A lot of selfish owners would probably be the first to complain if everyone started doing it and they had strange dogs fouling on their property.

Letting a dog out on to the street alone, even for a few minutes to relieve itself, is an offence. Over the last few years there has been a lot of publicity about dangerous dogs and attacks on the public, and as a result there is now more legislation concerning the general control of dogs. The law states that your dog must be under control in a public place at all times. Should an incident occur when it is not, especially if a person has been injured, then an owner can face a prison sentence, a hefty fine and/or the destruction of the dog.

If your dog is picked up by a dog warden, a fee is normally charged for its return, and if a particular dog is picked up more than once then the fee is often increased.

Dangerous dogs

Until 1991 there was only one Act of Parliament that dealt with dangerous dogs, the Dogs Act of 1871. Then came the Dangerous Dogs Act 1991, which was designed to give greater powers for dealing with such dogs. Under this Act, a complaint can be made to a magistrate that a dog is dangerous and/or not kept under proper control. A successful prosecution under this Act can result in a heavy fine or even imprisonment for the owner, and the destruction of the dog. This Act also means that a dog no longer has to injure anyone to be seized and the owner prosecuted, indeed the dog may not even be aggressive. A dog running in and out of heavy traffic could be said to be dangerously out of control. It has also meant that for the first time, magistrates can specify the type of control that an owner should use to control their dog. They can even order that a dog be neutered.

Guard dogs

The Guard Dogs Act of 1975 was passed as a result of a number of people being attacked by dogs that were guarding property. Under this law, a dog is considered a guard dog if 'It is being used to protect premises or property kept on a premises, or a person guarding a premises or such property.' This act also states that 'It is an offence to use, or permit the use of, a guard dog at any premises unless a person (handler) who is capable of controlling the dog is present on the premises, and the dog is under the control of the handler at all times while it is being used as a guard dog, except while it is secured so that it is not at liberty to roam the premises. The handler's duty to control the dog may only be relaxed if another handler capable of controlling it has control of it so that it cannot roam. A guard dog is not to be used at all unless a notice warning of its presence is clearly shown at each entrance to the premises.' Many dog owners simply have a pet dog, but have displayed in their windows such signs as 'Warning: guard dog loose'. Or 'No trespassing, remains will be prosecuted'. These signs are commonly sold in pet shops, and those who display them in their windows are clearly advertising that there is a guard dog present, or at least a very aggressive dog. This could render them liable to pay damages if a burglar breaks into their property and is bitten by a dog that was not properly controlled. Although this may sound incredible, I can assure you that it has already happened, so if you have any such sign, beware.

Dogs worrying livestock

The Protection of Livestock Act, 1953, states that if a dog worries livestock on any agricultural land, the owner or keeper of the dog is guilty of an offence. The owner of livestock that is being worried by a dog is legally entitled to take steps to prevent further worrying to his animals. This includes shooting the offending dog or dogs. Therefore it is extremely important that dogs are kept under the strictest control where domestic animals are about. Some of the animal rescue centres that have livestock animals that are used to dogs use them to acclimatize dogs to them. If you are planning a trip to the countryside and do not know how your dog will behave with such animals, it may be worth contacting your nearest rescue centre that has livestock and see if they operate such a service.

Breeding dogs

The Breeding of Dogs Act, 1973, requires owners of more than two breeding bitches, where the puppies are to be sold, to have a licence, usually obtainable from the local authority.

People often make the mistake of thinking that there are huge sums of money to be made in breeding dogs. This is often not the case. Yes, pedigree dogs can sell for a lot of money, but there are many costs involved in breeding dogs too, especially for the owner of the bitch. Firstly you will usually have to pay the owner of the dog a stud fee unless you also own the dog. Then you can expect the bitch's daily food intake to increase dramatically as the puppies are growing inside her, and absorbing more and more nutrients. This is often the point where the vet bills begin. Then as the puppies are born, it may be necessary to call the vet in if there are complications during the birth, or for the removal of dew-claws.

Once the puppies are born, again the bitch's appetite will increase, and so she will require more food. Then as the puppies are weaned they will have to be fed. As well as a puppy food, they will have to have powdered milk. They will also have to be wormed and possibly vaccinated. Then, if they are not sold quickly, their feeding requirements will increase, and you will still be feeding the mother, trying to get her back up to her normal condition.

Dogs that bite

The law is very clear on this matter: it is illegal for a dog to bite someone. The only exceptions are dogs in active service, such as police dogs, and even they should only use reasonable force or even the police can and have found themselves appearing in court – under a charge.

Even if someone breaks into your property, your dog is not allowed to bite them, and they are at liberty to prosecute you if your dog grabs hold of them as they are climbing out of the window carrying your video recorder.

All is not lost however. What punishment, if any, should be levied is at the magistrate's discretion. Many may choose not to punish the dog at all under the circumstances. People who have dogs in their shops behind the counter also need to beware about using the dog against thieves.

Part II

Re-educating the Troubled Dog

For some owners, all this preventative advice may have come too late. The dog has already developed behaviours that have created problems for it, and/or for the people with whom it comes into contact. To remedy this situation, some form of 're-education' of the dog needs to be carried out.

12 The Behavioural Interview

If a dog owner already has a problem that is too involved or serious for me to advise them over the phone, I will arrange to visit them and conduct an assessment interview. When I arrive for the interview, the first thing I usually try to do is to largely ignore the dog, and monitor how well it accepts this. I also often ask the owner to completely ignore the dog while I am there. This helps give me an idea of the relationship between the owner and the dog. This is the main reason that I like to go to the owner's address, rather than have them come to me. It gives me an opportunity to observe the dog in its own surroundings, where its behaviour may be completely different from its conduct in a strange environment. While I am discretely watching the dog, particularly while the owner is trying to ignore it, I am getting an indication as to how much control is being exerted by whom.

A recent fairly typical example involved a husband and wife and their very demanding dog that displayed both fear-based aggression and attention-seeking tendencies. I said to the owners, 'I want you both to ignore your dog while I'm here: don't speak to it, touch it or even look at it.'

You could almost see the blood draining from their faces at the horrifying concept of having to do this, showing how well their dog had trained them! After only a minute or so, the husband did give a furtive glance to the dog.

The wife shouted: 'Don't look at her.'

'I didn't!'

'Yes you did!'

And so it went on. This gave me an opportunity to observe the lengths the dog will go to in order to gain attention – the little control games that are going on between her and her owners. Just by studying the interaction or lack of it, we can begin to get an idea of what may be causing the problem.

Then I ask the owners to start working with me through a lengthy questionnaire. This enables me to gather in-depth information on the relationship between the dog and the owners, and its relationship with other dogs. I also learn how and where it eats and sleeps, its attitude to other family members and close family friends, the type of games that it likes to play, its response to grooming, and anything else that may be relevant. This enables me to build up a picture of the dog and its relationship with everything it encounters.

At first, owners often feel many of these things often seem to have no relation to the problem they are experiencing. However, once I give them an overall picture, they start to realize that certain things do contribute to it. I say what I think is causing the problem, and we discuss what can be done about it. I make it clear to the owners that in predatory pack animals, including man, there is normally a pack order of some description, a pack leader, a second-in-command, a third and so on, right down to the lowest ranking member of the group. In many human homes, the order begins with the father, then the mother (although this order frequently fluc-tuates), then the children, whose order varies according to age, strength, intelligence or a combination of these things. Lastly should come the dog. But sometimes, if it hasn't been made clear who the leaders are, the dog may try to work its way up in the pack. This often involves challenging those that it previously considered its superiors. The dog can become more difficult to control, as it no longer sees itself as subservient to the owners. It often becomes more disobedient, it can become destructive, and sometimes even aggressive.

I try to reinstate the family's position as pack leaders. This will improve the relationship between them and their dog, and increase their control over it. This will in turn increase their ability to teach the dog to respond reliably to whatever they are training it to do at that particular time.

These things by themselves will go a long way towards curing a lot of behavioural problems. I write them a programme to put right every problem that we recognized, and ask them to keep in regular contact with me. I like to hear how things are working out, whether certain measures need to be amended and, eventually, that all problems are solved.

13   Aggression

There are many types of aggression, fear-based, dominant, predatory and territorial to name but a few. The former is the most common problem. Owners who have inadvertently promoted their pet to the position of 'top dog' will have caused some aggression problems. Their dog generally has too high a status that leads him to believe that he can influence the behaviour of the human pack. This manifests itself as problems like dominant aggression, territorial aggression, and pack order aggression.

Fear-based Aggression

Cécile Curtis, the illustrator for this book, is a case in point.

Case History – The not entirely Great Dane

Merlin, Cécile's dog, had first shown a tendency towards fear-based aggression when he was a year old, but it was greatly exacerbated after being suddenly attacked from behind by a Rottweiler. This dog was off the lead and Cécile now knows he was of a dominant nature, and her dog was injured in the fight. After that, any male dog that so much as growled softly, or even glared at him, provoked an immediate response. This usually took the form of him breaking away from her (easily accomplished by a dog that is some ten pounds heavier than you are) and attacking the offender, although strangely it never resulted in any form of injury. By the time he was almost seven years old, she had become desperate and, even though she thought he might be too old to change, she finally contacted a local dog trainer who said she didn't need a trainer, but rather a behaviour consultant, and recommended me. After questioning me on previous cases, she was convinced to give it a try.

After carefully observing Cécile and her dog, my first instruction was that she always take some of her dog's favourite food treats with her on their walks, and the very instant that he saw another dog she was to give him some. This should start to make what had previously been a stressful experience into a more pleasant one. She also needed to work on the dog's general obedience, so that he would be more responsive to commands. Changing the dog's attitude towards other dogs was the most effective solution to what had become her greatest problem, and has revolutionized their daily outings. She seemed intensely relieved when I told her that Merlin's aggression was the fear-based kind and not the dominant type, which she had suspected.

I also learned that she was an artist and author, and it was not long after this that we discussed plans to collaborate on this book.

Fear-based aggression can be caused by such a variety of complex situations that at times, the behaviourist has to be a detective as well as a canine consultant.

Case History – The mystery of the teetotal retriever

This Labrador Retriever came to my training class when he was about eight or nine months old. He had a good temperament, and seemingly loved everybody. After a few months, his owners were concerned that he'd start to become very agitated and bark furiously at certain people for no apparent reason. I asked them to keep a record of all those individuals – as complete a physical description as possible, whether they were carrying anything, their height, colouring, what they were wearing, how quickly they were moving and so on. The woman did this for a couple of weeks, then came back and said her dog showed no pattern whatsoever. She tried to get him to take food from various people chosen at random. Naturally the dog loved this, but when he did bark at someone, there was no time to give them titbits to offer him beforehand.

Time passed without any significant progress, and then one day at my training class, the dog started barking in a very stressful manner at me. He had always got on very well with me and would even drag his owner over to greet me. We were really baffled by this sudden change, but as I moved away from the dog, I realized that he had not been barking at me at all, but at a man who'd been standing directly behind me. This man was always a little dishevelled and was well known for enjoying more than the occasional tipple, and people had often commented that they could smell alcohol on him. It was at that moment that a tiny light bulb flashed on inside my head. I knew that the owner's husband also enjoyed a drink, so I asked her if they ever took their dog to a pub. She said they did, and for a while he was well behaved, although several intoxicated customers had stepped on him at times and in addition, the pub dog had also had a go at him, adding insult to injury! He was no longer keen to go there any more. It seemed that I had found the answer.

I asked the owners if they could ask anyone at whom he barked if they'd recently had a drink. In every case, they said that they had and, sure enough, the dog had learned to associate these people with something unpleasant, which he believed was likely to happen whenever he was around people who had been drinking. Being able to detect this threat from thirty to forty feet, depending on wind direction, his fear had continued to increase, and would eventually have led to more aggression. He may well have bitten someone. Dogs will also pick up on anyone who is behaving in a drunken or erratic manner, and if it's not dealt with, this behaviour often escalates until it becomes phobic.

To cure the dog, I used a method called desensitization. It involves exposing the dog to the stress stimulus at a sufficiently low level that the dog acknowledges the threat, but can just cope with that level. A huge reward is attached for ignoring or interacting with it. You then gradually increase the level of exposure. The dog gets progressively more used to the stimulus until eventually, it finds that stimulus rewarding rather than fear-inducing. So what they did was to take the dog relatively near to the pub and ask people who were leaving to throw him titbits at a distance. Over a period of time, as the dog got used to being fed by strangers who smelled of alcohol, the owners then moved him gradually closer and closer and eventually had people feeding him by hand and patting him. It's very important the dog gets the rewards from the people who actually caused the stress if that is possible. It took about three weeks to work out this problem.

The typical fearful dog, such as Cécile's Great Dane, has learned that, by making lots of noise and flying at another dog to intimidate it, the other dog often won't attack. Dogs may also believe that their owner will pull the two dogs apart and this can be a way to avoid ending up in a fight. The next most common misapprehension is that people always assume that if their dog runs after another who's heading in the opposite direction, say, fifty yards away, it must be dominant aggressive because otherwise, why would it go for this one which was nowhere near it? I believe that what he is doing is ensuring that there won't be a fight with the other dog. If you talk to the owner of one of these dogs, he will usually say, 'Oh yes, he steams into the other one, I swear he'd kill it if he could!' But if you ask if he's ever actually injured any other dog, the answer is frequently, 'No, but only because I ran about fifty yards and got him before he could.'

In the time that took, the two will have been fighting for several minutes, and yet there usually isn't a mark on either dog. Why? If he really wanted to hurt the other dog, why does he always fail to do so? I do not believe that was what the attack was about. Rather, it was about driving the other dog away, and once you call him, he will come back very readily because he actually never wanted to fight in the first place. What he wanted was for you to get hold of him and for the other owner to grab his dog and take it away, so what your dog did was to ensure that the other dog wouldn't come back. What he probably learned in the past is: 'Yes, I've seen the other dog going off in another direction and turn around to come back on me again and suddenly, it's right behind me – so this way, I can ensure that won't happen.' This is a sure sign of fear-based behaviour. German Shepherd Dogs tend to charge the other dog and bowl it over, usually hitting it sideways on and sending it rolling. The other dog screams and runs off. Clearly, this is not a dog who is trying to injure another one who had just rolled over and run away. This is *not* a dominant dog. The next section discusses dogs that are.

In summary:

1 Never buy a puppy if either of its parents show signs of aggression when you go to visit them. If the mother has to be locked away when you arrive, steer clear of these puppies also. Chances are that the puppies will have learnt to be frightened of visitors by that time from their parents, and will exhibit that behaviour as they get older, even if they are not showing it when you first see them.

2 When you bring your puppy home, try to let him experience as many things as possible, even before he has had his vaccinations. Carry him out with you to the local shops, so that he experiences traffic, strangers, and all the other sights and sounds of the outdoors. The most important socialization period in a puppy's life is up to the age of thirteen weeks, and if your puppy hasn't experienced enough of these things by that age, you will probably have problems getting him to accept them as he gets older. You can tape sounds that may be stressful to him when he first goes out and hears them for the first time, such as traffic and trains. Play the tape indoors before he is vaccinated, so that by the time that he is able to go out, he is already familiar with these noises, and so is less likely to react badly to them.

3 Do not allow your puppy to be bullied or intimidated by larger, older dogs while he is little. The vast number of people who own a dog that is fearful of other dogs as an adult will tell a story of how it was attacked by a fully grown dog while it was a puppy.

4 If you have a dog that is already fearful of other dogs, do not allow it to practise fighting techniques on dogs that it *is* friendly with. The more that it practises, the better a fighter it will become, and the more aggressive it will be towards other dogs. Instead, use a toy or food reward to encourage the dog to be less interested in other dogs, and more interested in interacting with you.

5 If your dog is fearful of traffic or people that it encounters on walks, you will need to change the dog's association with that stimulus, so that it regards it as potentially rewarding.

Dominant Aggression

This is a most serious form of aggression, and a great many people, especially those who are not very experienced, mistake other forms of aggression for dominant. A dominant aggressive dog is usually a very quiet animal, one who does not make a lot of threatening noises. The dog that is dominant and about to bite somebody, apart from perhaps a little low growling, generally gives no audible signs that it is about to be aggressive.

Case History – Go ahead, make my day

I had been called out to the home of a woman whose German Shepherd had prompted many complaints in the neighbourhood. The dog barked excessively, and chased after anyone she saw that moved or showed fear of her, a good example of fear-based aggression. I was there primarily in my capacity as a dog warden, not as a behaviourist, and was accompanied by the senior animal welfare officer. We went in, sat down in the living room and were just about to discuss the problems concerning this dog, when a gigantic male Rottweiler appeared from nowhere. He walked up to the chair in which my colleague was sitting, and jumped up on it, putting his paws on the front of her seat. He was facing her off, half an inch from the end of her nose, staring straight into her eyes as though boring into the back of her head. He was basically daring her to move. 'Give me a reason and I'll have your face off!' he said. She asked me in a whispered voice what she should do. I told her to turn her face away, ever so slowly, because he was trying to force eye contact. If she looked at him for any longer than he was happy with, he would think, 'OK, you've accepted my challenge, 'ave some o' this!'

She said, 'Suppose he bites me?' I told her at that point it didn't matter how he got hold of her. Whether it was the side of her face or the front, if he meant to get her, he was going to, so it was not a good idea to encourage him. She then turned her head and he tried to follow it around, attempting to maintain the eye contact.

This continued, until after a few seconds he got off her chair, came over and repeated the process with me. I did the same thing as she had done, and he seemed to say, 'Right, fine, you both know the rules.' With this he got down again, made a slow exit from the room and we never saw him again. His message had been conveyed: 'You've come into my territory, let me make sure that you are very submissive, otherwise I'll have to teach you to be.' Dogs regard staring as a challenge, so when in doubt, look away.

The moral of this cautionary tale would also seem to be: 'Beware of the dog that doesn't bark!' The owner had no idea how to deal with her dog's aggression, so, like many owners, she tried to convince herself that he wasn't really aggressive at all. Prior to his arrival, we did not know she had two dogs. What had happened in the past was that the Rottweiler was permanently kept out in the garden as a guard dog, but on this occasion, the children had accidentally let him in. There was no conflict between him and the Shepherd, as the latter was a bitch and knew better. Of course, he was the dominant animal in that home and everyone in the family acknowledged him as such. But obviously, it was a very dangerous situation.

The owners would find it difficult to retake control of this dog because he was supremely confident of his position as pack leader. Added to this, the whole family was afraid of him, and he knew it. Castration may help to make him less 'macho' generally, but this would not cure him by itself. They would have to try to lower his position.

Unfortunately, the Rottweiler was not re-trained. Incredibly, the owners wanted him to be aggressive as they considered him to be their guard dog. I explained that a guard dog is under the control of its owners, whereas no one could in fact control or significantly affect the Rottweiler's behaviour. However, his owners were unmoving.

I am constantly amazed by the extreme forms of bad behaviour and aggression that dog owners will tolerate, and for which they will find excuses and sometimes try to work around. Yet what often prompts them to contact me is some other behaviour I consider relatively minor.

Case History – Who wears the trousers?

The owners of a Border Terrier wanted to consult me about its habit of chewing up the post. As I was going to be in that very street the same day, I said I'd stop by for a quick chat. It turned out to be anything but quick. They started the interview by saying that their 8-year-old dog had been, for almost the entire time they'd had it, aggressive towards other dogs as well as children, and would go for anyone at all who leaned over it, which included them and their family. It had bitten several people, it fouled and urinated indoors – usually in the upstairs hallways – and it barked incessantly at anything that moved in the garden, arousing bitter complaints from the neighbours about the noise. In addition to this, it was the most exasperating attention-seeker and would insist on making someone respond to it. They had problems getting it out of bedrooms and could not get it off the furniture – yet the only reason they felt the need to contact me was that they couldn't stop it chewing the post! Everything else they found excuses for, saying, 'He's fearful – oh well, he's had a hard time.' (Even though they got him at eight weeks old!) It's incredible that they didn't view these other things as problems!

Another thing I've observed is that some dogs have actually been taught to use aggression to get what they want, if inadvertently. For example, the young puppy is bored to tears while everyone is watching their favourite TV soap and it's looking for something to do, so it rushes up to someone and bites their ankle. They immediately stop looking at the television, grab the dog's most treasured toy and encourage him to play with it. Unfortunately, what the puppy realizes is that biting someone is an excellent way to get attention.

Something I think people must understand is that puppies, or dogs, don't 'nip', and they don't 'play bite' or 'mouth', or any of these sort of terms that people use. A dog that intentionally laid his teeth on you has bitten you, and this is something owners need to recognize. It is important not to start making excuses for what it has done. What the dog is then learning is that under certain circumstances – those that *it* decides – it's acceptable behaviour to bite people and you don't want your dog *ever* to think that.

What happens with a puppy is that owners start to play with it to distract it, and as it grows older, it learns that biting is a very good way to make them interact with it. It works very well indeed!

As it gets bigger, the dog continues to bite and it hurts more and more. After a year and a half or so, the owners start doing things to avoid this, for example, sitting with toys in their laps whilst watching the television, to encourage the dog to play with the toy instead of its owner. Thus the dog has learned to control them in any environment and they have ended up with an ever-increasing problem, which starts to get dreadfully out of hand. Unfortunately, they usually leave it far too long, by which time their dog is a seasoned biter and it's much harder to cure.

You should be aware that when your puppy is six weeks old and you've just brought it home, you have got to start to teach it then that biting is out! The remedy is to deliberately do things that would annoy it. For example, when you put its food down, if you start to put your hand in its bowl and it growls or so much as makes a noise, you should grab it by the scruff of the neck and shake it, just the way its mother would do – really aggressively. Shout as though you were absolutely furious. What the puppy will learn at a very early age is that he must never use aggression against these people, because the level they can use is far superior to his. If you leave it too late, unfortunately the growing puppy thinks it's all right to bite back, and then it's too big for you to shake it. If you try to 'scruff' that dog, the chances are its going to go for you, because it's already confidently using aggression. When you start suddenly trying to use it back, it's not going to take it very well.

Case History – Do not feed the spaniel!

One such case concerned a 4-year-old male Springer Spaniel. The owner had got him when he was a young puppy from a breeder when he was just a typical, lovely, ordinary, everyday puppy. The man who owned him worked in a mechanics garage, and used to take the dog to work with him every day. It had a kennel there, but he had to chain it to avoid it running about in the yard. It still had about six or seven feet in every direction. All the other staff would play with it and give it food, and there was a woman who used to come every morning with a biscuit when she passed.

One day, it took the biscuit and then flew out and bit her hand. This was the first time the owner could recall having noticed any aggression from the dog. Often the case is that there are other signs, but an owner just doesn't recognize them as such. Later he noticed that it would chase some of the staff as they walked by, running out and grabbing them by the ankles, but no one was too concerned about this as the dog was only young. Gradually the bites got harder and harder, the aggression increasing, until one day it pinned one of the staff to the bonnet of a car, snarling into his face. At this point the manager said it would be best if he didn't bring the dog to work anymore. So he left it at home, starting off by leaving it the run of the house. But every time that he and his wife were about to come back in, the dog would hurl himself at the front door, growling and snarling, even though they'd advertised the fact that it was only them!

The aggression had obviously escalated, so they moved the dog to the kitchen which had stable-type doors, the top of which was left open, the lower half being about four feet high. When the owner contacted me, he asked if I would meet him outside his house so he could show me what happened when he entered his front door, arriving home from work. I met him at the doorstep and, after he announced that it was he, we entered, and all we could see was a set of teeth as it tried to hurl itself over the top. He then put it in the back garden, following his usual procedure – moving the door slowly open, shouting at the dog as he did so. It then gave the same treatment to the back door as it shot out into the garden and began to tear chunks out of everything there. Every bush, tree, every clump of grass was attacked in a state of utter frustration. Finally, the dog flew back at the door which the man had slammed shut, leaving the dog snarling outside it. This was also normal, I was told.

So we sat down and started to work our way through the programme. It became apparent that this dog had bitten him and his wife on many occasions, usually over things like being too slow to move away after they put his food down, in which case he would fly at them. If they tried to sit in a chair the dog was in, he would bite them, or if they moved too suddenly, they'd be bitten. When they went to enter their bedroom while the dog was in it, he would leap towards them aggressively so they had to get him out of the room first, offering him food treats.

Unbelievably, this had been going on now for a couple of years! Every time anyone came to see them, the dog had to be locked away. It had not seen any visitors during the past two years because the couple were so fearful of what it would do if they came in the house.

When we had got through the questionnaire, I asked the man to let the dog into the room. He was most reluctant to do so, but I assured him that it was just to see what the dog would do. As it turned out, this wasn't a very wise thing to do. If I had known then what I know now, I probably wouldn't have done it. The dog entered the room and walked slowly past me into the centre of the room, picked up an old training shoe which was apparently his, lay down on the floor and began to chew it, all the while staring directly at me. We carried on talking but the owner was clearly very stressed and concerned. However, we tried to continue as though the dog were not present. But he soon made it clear that ignoring him was unacceptable, and would not be tolerated. He slowly stood and began the most almighty roaring I had heard from a dog for some considerable time. I continued to talk to the owner as though the dog were not in the room, but the owner was now in a state of near-panic. He asked me what he should do now. I told him that the most important thing now was that neither of us move from our present positions, as if we did, this would almost certainly galvanize the dog into attacking.

He continued this tirade of canine abuse for a minute or so, then stopped, picked up his shoe and calmly left the room. A couple of minutes later he returned, still carrying the shoe. He crossed the room again, dragging his body over my legs as he passed, and lay down in the same place as before. After a couple of minutes, he repeated the previous ritual, except that this time, instead of standing in the middle of the room roaring at me, he approached me and stood with his head over the arm of my chair. The swearing lasted longer this time, the dog stepping up his level of aggression, trying to force a response. But still neither of us moved. Finally the dog again stopped barking, took his shoe and left the room.

This time, however, he returned after only a minute or so, again crossing over my legs and returning to his earlier position. Yet again he started shouting doggie profanities at me, but on this occasion he actually put his front paws on the arm of my chair and growled and snarled into my face.

The whole situation had changed. The warning was now far more direct, with the dog making it clear that he was fast losing patience with this refusal to submit on my part. He clearly felt that he was going to have to teach me proper manners, which for him meant waiting for me to do something that allowed him the pleasure of biting me. At this point I advised the owner to shut the dog out after it left the room, which he was only too glad to do. As soon as the door was closed, the dog realized that it had been shut out and threw itself against the door in an absolute fury. The owner said that this was how it always behaved if you denied it access to a room.

One of my biggest concerns with this situation was that the man's wife was eight months' pregnant, and I was totally convinced that at least one of them, including the baby once it was born, was likely to be very seriously injured by this dog. Without any guilt or apprehension, I advised the man that the only thing to do was to put the dog to sleep, because I could not safely run a programme which would not involve him attacking someone later on, and I certainly don't ever want that on my conscience.

Another case of dangerous aggression was that of idiopathic aggression (aggression for no apparent reason) in an English Bull Terrier.

Case History – Mad Max

I first saw Max when he was about four or five months old, being walked by his owner in the local park. He seemed very friendly, wanting to investigate everything and eager to play with everybody. If I had to say he had any problem, it would have been that he was unresponsive to the owner's commands or to coming back when called, but the owner seemed content to follow the dog around the park. As the dog got older, this was becoming more apparent. He was finding it increasingly difficult to get Max to come to him, and became more aggressive towards the dog in his attempts to make it do so. He would shout at him, without much effect. By the time Max had reached eighteen months or so, I noticed he was keeping him on the lead a lot, suggesting that he had become even less responsive, or perhaps more aggressive. This often happens when dogs spend too much time playing with others when they're young – they eventually end up being aggressive to them having had so many opportunities to practise. I wasn't terribly surprised that he now kept the dog on a lead.

By the time this dog reached two and a half or three, I was asked by our local vet to go and have a look at him. The owner had gone to the vet complaining of aggression. When I went to visit the owner's house, the dog was in the garden. The owner and I sat in his living-room, which faced onto the patio, and I asked him to give an example of the dog's behaviour. He said that he would show me. He went up to the patio doors, which had the curtains drawn, and called the dog's name. Suddenly, there came an almighty roaring and snarling from the other side of the door. He explained that this was what Max was like now if he made any attempt to interact with him – complete ferocity. He had to throw the dog's food out of the window, and could not go out in the garden at all. There was no question of touching him or stroking him or taking him for a walk, because he wouldn't let him near enough even to put a lead on. Max now lived in the shed, and contact between them was utterly impossible. The owner was quite certain that if he made any move in his direction, the dog would attack unreservedly.

After having talked to the man at great length, it became apparent that I couldn't reasonably ask him to do anything with his dog to change the behaviour. He would definitely be at great risk. Curiously enough, the only other times I had been called to visit English Bull Terriers, they always had one common problem – aggression towards their owners. I did however find it strange that this one had become so aggressive over such a short period of time, when the owner didn't appear to have done anything to cause it. He hadn't been frightened by the dog, nor in any way intimidated by him up to this point, but he said the aggression seemed to have occurred almost overnight, when the dog had suddenly started flying at him. So he put the dog in the garden as a punishment, something that he had done many times before. There had never been any form of aggressive response from the dog on any previous occasion. But this time, when he went to let the dog back in, it wouldn't allow him to open the door. This had been going on for several weeks.

I'm not sure what caused such aggression – it didn't seem to have any apparent motive, but the dog had taken it absolutely to the extreme. Perhaps the cause was physical, a brain tumour maybe, but as far as the owner was concerned, there was only one option. There was no way in which I would have been prepared to risk that dog attacking his owner, because I believed that if it had ever got hold of him, it was certainly capable of causing serious injury. The owner was not really prepared to try to work at curing the dog either, as he no longer liked or trusted it. So this was one of the rare cases when I had to tell an owner to have a dog put to sleep.

I recall a dog I knew in my childhood that would have been a behaviourist's nightmare. This dog was a mongrel named Remi, which was short for Remington. He had the kind of assortment of behavioural problems that make most psychologists shudder. For starters, he was dreadfully over-sexed – clearly not caring to whom or what he made amorous advances, even his own puppies, towards which he would just as easily turn dangerously aggressive at the drop of a hat. He was basically a bully who used aggression to intimidate, and was very successful in this endeavour, and the family he permitted to share *his* house (as he saw it) were all afraid of him. The family also owned a bitch, but she showed little interest in her puppies, even before they were fully weaned. She certainly showed no maternal instinct or desire to protect them from him. Indeed in hind-sight I do not understand why the dogs were allowed to breed, or why Remi wasn't castrated, as this may have helped with some of his other behavioural problems. Remi had on many occasions attacked the bitch, an unusual trait in a male dog, and she had learnt to give him a wide berth wherever possible. The family also often tried to keep them apart, and frequently had to intervene when fights broke out.

He was also food aggressive, and would turn on anyone who was foolish enough to disturb him while he was eating. He would protect his bed, and resented anyone approaching it, even if he wasn't in it. If he was in it, everyone knew to steer clear.

Remi's aggression increased to the point where the bitch and several of the puppies had to be rehomed. The family later acquired a second bitch, a rescue with a dreadful hair loss problem. She was, almost from the start, completely intolerant of the remaining puppies, so they too were rehoused, which looking back was undoubtedly the best thing for them. Ironically, this second bitch ended up ruling the roost to such an extent that Remi had to take a back seat to her. As she asserted herself more and more, so Remi seemed to shrink into himself. His condition began to deteriorate, until he was completely humbled by her. The last time that I saw them, which was many years ago, Remi was a rather pathetic shadow of his former self, while the bitch still kept him firmly in his place.

This is a good example of a case where an expert should have been called in to deal with this situation before it ever got so far out of hand.

In summary:

1 Ensure that the dog never has a status that puts him over anyone that lives in, or is invited into your house.
2 If your dog has dominant tendencies, do not allow it to do things that boost its position further, such as sleeping in the bedroom, feeding before or at the same time as the humans, or pulling on the lead to put itself in front of you so it leads you on walks. Also do not allow it to lead you through doorways.
3 You may find that neutering the dog will help to lower its status, but this in itself will be unlikely to cure the dog.

Territorial Aggression

Case History – Possession is nine-tenths of the law!

The owner of a haulage firm contacted me recently in my capacity as an animal welfare officer. A close neighbour of his owned two German Shepherds, which were only very rarely exercised. The result was that the dogs were very protective towards their property, as they saw little else.

One day, a section of the dog owner's fence came down, and the two dogs escaped. After roaming locally for a short while, they headed back for home, but in order to get there, they had to pass the entrance to the lorry yard. As they were passing, one of the dogs noticed a lorry with the door open. As both dogs loved to go out in their owner's transit van, they appeared to decide that this lorry was the next best thing, so in they jumped.

Picture the expression of the driver when he returned and hopped up into the cab of his lorry, to be confronted by two very angry Shepherds who think that he is trespassing in *their* van. Blind terror! Before the dogs had even noticed that he had gone, the driver was in the office getting the owner of the company to ring me.

When I arrived, the dogs had made themselves comfortable on the front seat, and although the door was still open, they clearly had no intention of moving. The dogs didn't mind anyone standing in the doorway, but they were not letting anyone into the lorry. They had now been in the lorry for a couple of hours, so I figured that they were probably hungry by now. I produced a bag of dog treats, and threw a couple to the dog that was nearest to me. He grabbed them greedily. The other dog pushed its way forward, trying to get a share of the food. It was then a simple matter of getting them to follow the food out of the van, and, using the food as a lure, putting leads on them.

By their very nature, dogs guard. Some barking at strangers or unexpected noises is often considered a good thing, while too much is not. Dog owners are often faced with the problem of over-reaction by their dogs. But this 'guarding instinct' is controllable. When my dogs bark in normal circumstances, I have trained them to understand that four barks each is acceptable, and to carry on after that is not. To achieve this, I simply verbally rewarded them for the first four barks, then if they carried on with a fifth, I would command them to be quiet, and not allow them to bark any more. They gradually came to realize that approximately four barks was a level of barking that was acceptable. It is not an exact science, and they may bark three or five times, but they have understood that they are not allowed to bark continually. The regular appearances of milkmen or postmen present a threat to the territorially aggressive dog, the latter in particular, as they not only come to the door, but they push something through it, which appears to be even more threatening and invasive. After a sharp canine reprimand, these people go away, so it works on them. The trouble is, they inevitably come back again the next day! I have often had to deal with this problem in cases where the dog becomes extremely aggressive, and their owners, frantic. It also accounts for the fact that many postmen are very wary of dogs!

This type of aggression can be confused with the fear-based variety, which in turn can be mistaken for dominant aggression. It is the behaviourist's function to discover from the owners what circumstances spark off unacceptable practices and then treat these accordingly.

Often, owners have said to me, 'Oh, my dog's normally

friendly with everyone, but when he sees the postman, he goes mad!' Of course, if a postman put a tasty titbit through the door of every home when he had to approach it, this problem could soon be solved, but this might be somewhat difficult to organize. The most commonly employed solution is to install a basket on the other side of the letterbox, so that the postman cannot be bitten. In accordance with the Dangerous Dogs Act, it is an offence for an animal even to unreasonably put people into a state of fear and if it actually bites, the owner is in a great deal of trouble.

Another example of territorial aggression is when a dog is completely friendly, except when it is in a car. The reason for this may be that this is the only place where they are completely free to see everything going on around them, added to it being such a small space to defend. I did a programme for a Rough Collie who was fine with everyone else except his owner, showing him extreme aggression, but after having cured that problem, I was again consulted when he became very aggressive to anyone who came anywhere near 'his' car.

Case History – Who needs a car alarm?

This case involved a rescued dog, a Miniature Schnauzer, who, judging by his initial behaviour, had probably rarely, if ever, been in a car before. His new owners had had him for about six months when this new trait appeared. By the time they again contacted me, it was a case of when anyone came near the stationary car, be it a cyclist, or pedestrian walking past, he went absolutely berserk, hurling himself at the window, snarling and growling. The situation was further complicated by the fact that he was an otherwise very appealing-looking affectionate dog, and when people saw him in passing, they came over to say hello, at which he instantly reverted to extreme aggression – all teeth!

His owners had become deeply concerned as their car was a saloon, without the facility to put a dog guard at the back seat. It became particularly dangerous when the car was in motion, as their dog was free to come forward between the front seats and almost reach the windscreen. When they stopped he would immediately become quiet and then start up again when they moved. The trouble was he got the impression he was only being punished for being quiet, as he had always stopped barking by the time they stopped the car and got to him! What they needed was a means of control. I recommended they put him on a very long lead, enabling the passenger to check him firmly, telling him to be quiet, whenever he started to bark. So, very quickly he realized he was being controlled even while in the back seat. They were even able to control him when people passed the parked vehicle. The combination of these two solutions cured the dog. This was certainly a case of one who had taken territorial aggression a bit too far!

Difficulties can arise when there is evidence of more than one type of aggression. A Border Collie for whom I did a programme recently was a good example. At fourteen months old it was showing dominant aggression towards its owners, fear-based aggression towards other people, while outside it had a very high predatory aggression and would chase anything that was moving rapidly, and in addition to all that, had a strong territorial aggression, being very controlling with anyone who came onto their property. He was extremely protective of the car and even of his own lead when wearing it. If one replaced it with another one, he immediately became calmer.

In summary:

1 Keep your dog's status within the pack sufficiently low that the dog doesn't feel that it is his right to be the sole defender of the territory. Your dog should accept that if the owner is not being aggressive, then there is no need for him to be either.
2 You can use sound deterrents such as a can with pebbles in it to stop your dog from chasing or being excessive in its aggression if you cannot control it by voice alone.
3 Try to change your dog's attitude to the stimuli that cause its aggression, perhaps by encouraging people like the postman to drop a food treat through the letterbox before putting the letters through.

Food Aggression

It's important to remember that one dog can show several forms of aggression. However, here is an example that revolved entirely around food. The solution to the problem again involved 're-education'.

Case history – One bowl of food for me . . . and one for Me

We had a litter of Labrador puppies which we rehomed, and at about six months, one became particularly aggressive over things it considered to be its own, especially food. I had advised its owners about measures they could employ to get it over this, but unfortunately, they didn't do any of these things, figuring that he would grow out of it. About three months later, they contacted me to say that this puppy had attacked the husband and badly bitten his arm, and he no longer wished to keep the dog. When we picked it up, we found that it really did have an unusually high food aggression, and would not let anyone near it while it was eating. I had to put the dog through a programme to desensitize it to food which took a total of six weeks at our kennels, until we got to the stage where it would actually back away from food if anyone approached it.

There was no use of aggression on our part. We simply started off feeding it on very bland, dry biscuit mixer and had the dog on a long line. We would then pull the dog away from it and every time we did this, we added a very tasty morsel of food to the bowl on top of the meal. As soon as it had eaten the nice bit, we pulled the dog away again, placing more small quantities of tempting food on top. Very quickly, he learned that it was profitable to back away from his bowl

when anyone approached it, and this he would do. Once we had achieved this, we were able to rehome him without any worries regarding his being food aggressive, and to our knowledge he never was again.

This illustrates that these problems *are* curable: you just need to make sure you realize what the problem is, and then get the right advice on how to cure it.

Food aggression can be a real problem. It appears to be most commonly found in gundogs, and is especially in evidence when giving them bones. They can be particularly aggressive over these, as they are something more special, something to be more protective about, as they don't get them very often.

The methods of treating it are very much dependent upon the behavioural pattern of the dog, and the circumstances in which it shows the aggression. In cases of food aggression, one needs to contact an expert to discover the best remedy.

Case History – This Cocker Spaniel is *no* lady!

A man contacted me because he was having problems with the family dog around meal-times. In this household, it was the wife's job to feed the dog. When she was preparing the dog's food, which was the dried variety and needed time to soak, the dog would lie across the doorway, and allow no one else to enter the kitchen. If the wife left the room, only she would be allowed back into it. While this was bad enough, the family had learnt to cope with the dog's control over feeding rites. However, the final straw came when the dog did what so many dogs do in a situation where they are succeeding in getting away with something that everyone, including them, knows they shouldn't have got away with. The dog takes things a stage further.

What the dog started to do then was make demands at the *family*'s meal-times. What she began to do was lie by the dining table, and as the wife served dinner, the dog would patrol around the table, and not let the husband or the son sit down. So they worked out that they had to sit down before the food was put on the table. Again, the dog figured a way around this, and started to lie under the table as soon as the wife started cooking. So the husband and son had to sit at the table before the wife began to cook, and couldn't get up again, or the dog wouldn't let them come back again. They decided enough was enough, and contacted me.

To re-train this dog, we needed to make food less of a commodity. So instead of having only one food bowl, the dog had three bowls in the living room, three in the dining room, and three in the kitchen. All of the bowls were put in different areas of each room. The dog would be fed in a different room each meal-time, with a small amount of food being placed in each bowl. I also passed a rule that the wife was no longer allowed to feed the dog. This would help to improve the dog's relationship with the father and son. We taught the dog to be respectful by using a sound deterrent (see p.177), in conjunction with a long line attached to the dog's collar. These measures ensured that the dog was never allowed near the table while they were eating.

To summarize, always be the one to control the dog's food, rather than letting the dog take control. If you have a dog with dominant tendencies, do not always feed it at the same time. Regular meal-times encourage the dog to demand to be fed, often a little earlier each day, and the owner usually responds, jumping up to feed it as the dog is telling them it is hungry. Never give in to demands for extra food. If you know that the dog has had its correct amount, and he tells you that he wants more – *hard luck*. It is not in his best interests health-wise, and you will be creating a monster if you let him think that he has that much power over you. And if he stands by the biscuit jar whining, let him whine. He will eventually realize that he is not in control, and that you will only give him a biscuit when *you* want to, preferably because he has earned a reward for something that he has done well.

Never be tempted to feed your dog from your plate. I know that he is sitting there slavering, looking for all the world as though he hasn't seen food in weeks, and as though he's dying of starvation, but what he is doing is trying to gain access to the pack leader's food, which helps elevate his status to the same as yours. Instead, any leftovers that you may wish to give him should be put to one side, and given to him at his own meal-time.

Pack Order Aggression

This is another form of aggression seen in many different pack animals, including dogs. It is a kind of 'pecking order' aggression, found where there is more than one dog. It is even more common when there are more than two, as two will often co-exist, but three may form alliances against each other, and one dog, feeling it has the support of another, will bully the third. It can also appear in a family where there is only one dog, and it is in this situation that owners often misconstrue what is actually occurring.

Case History – And Daddy makes three (one too many)

Life in this house totally revolved around the dominant aggressive Dandie Dinmont. Again, he was a present for the wife, who had spoilt him relentlessly. He slept not just on the bed, but in it – under the duvet. The husband noticed that he invariably ended up teetering on the edge of the bed while the dog moved into what had been his place. He was stroked, hugged and kissed constantly by the wife. He always ate the same food as them, on a plate of course. He had access to all of the furniture. It was clear that if both owners were drowning, and it fell to the dog to save only one of them, Dad was a goner! The funny thing was if the husband and the dog were drowning, and the wife could save either the dog or her husband, I think the outcome would have been the same. No wonder he was aggressive.

By simply trying to cure the possessive attitude towards certain areas of the home, they thought that this would cure the aggression, but without curing the greater problem, which was the dominance, the situation continued.

In cases like this one, you usually find that by addressing the root of the problem, many of the other things that are happening as symptoms of that disappear. It is being able to recognize and treat that core problem that many owners, and sometimes even 'dog trainers', find difficult unless they have a comprehensive understanding of dog behaviour, which is all too often not the case. This is something that I have become fully aware of as, some years ago, I was guilty of it myself. But times and methods change, and what was once accepted as the best way to deal with a problem is not necessarily still true. You have to be flexible and adapt your instruction for the individual. You can only do this if you can accurately diagnose the condition. For example, I was talking to a fellow dog trainer who had visited my class one evening. She commented on a German Shepherd in the hall that was very fearful of other dogs and some people, and was barking at any dog that approached it. We had been offering it food treats to teach it to relax in the environment before we would attempt to work it in a room full of noisy dogs, when she came and spoke to me about this particular dog.

'I don't know why you're wasting time mucking about with treats and toys with that dog,' she said. 'There's a much quicker way to cure it.'

'And what would you suggest?' I asked, already knowing what she would say.

'I'd put a check chain on it, right up behind its ears, and every time it barked, I'd check its head off,' she replied.

This is a good example of a dog trainer completely misunderstanding what a dog is trying to say. Her remedy, based on this misunderstanding, would hugely increase the likelihood of the dog causing injury to someone or something. What the trainer thought the dog was saying was, 'Come here and let me have a go at you, as I am really dominant and want to lead this pack.' But what it was actually saying was, 'I am very frightened of you, so if I pretend to be big and tough, you might be scared enough to leave me alone.' So let's imagine that I took her advice and stopped the dog barking and giving warnings to stay away, but did nothing to reduce the dog's fear. People would think that the dog was no longer aggressive and would start approaching it. The dog would continue to get more and more frightened, and more stressed as it can no longer tell everyone to stay away, and by punishing it, you only give it one more unpleasant association with the presence of other people and dogs. The outcome is inevitable. Eventually there is an explosion of aggression from the dog, but this time the level of aggression that the dog uses is enough to get it put to sleep. Ironically enough, the same instructor ended up rehoming her own dog, because she found that she couldn't train it, as he would not respond to the training methods she was using.

A colleague, John Rogerson, whose guidance had been requested by another behaviourist, originally recited a rather unusual example of pack aggression to me.

Case History – United we stand . . .

This occurred with a woman who owned two terriers. She and her husband were elderly, and problems began when he was admitted to hospital. While he was away, the dogs suddenly began fighting each other. The wife would then have to try to separate them, but although the dogs never seemed to do each other any serious injury, she would always get badly bitten trying to get them apart. As they seemed to be fighting for dominance, she was advised to separate them as much as possible, keeping the more dominant one upstairs. But both dogs were miserable when parted, and howled continually to be reunited. She tried swapping them around, but it made no difference. She then tried keeping them both together, with one dog caged to stop them from fighting. Still they cried and whined for each other, so she released the caged one again, but it was not long before the fighting resumed.

The reason behind this aggression was most unexpected. What had happened was that the dogs had decided, in the absence of the husband, that while neither of them felt confident enough to challenge the wife for pack leadership on its own, they believed that as a coalition they would have the combined strength to overthrow her and lead the pack. So their strategy was to start a fight, which would often be set on or around furniture, which they would bite during these brawls, as it was guaranteed to get her involved. As soon as she got in the middle, she was attacked very aggressively, to put her in her place. This was why the dogs never injured each other, as that was never their intention. It simply provided them with an opportunity to attack her!

Once John realized what the dogs' intentions were, he was able to advise the behaviourist on how to put the problem right. What the owner had to do was to ensure that she was promoted above the dogs. She was never to interfere if the dogs started fighting. On the contrary, she was to leave the room and shut the door, leaving them to get on with it. She was to practise making the dogs more responsive to commands, and only feed them after they had performed an obedience exercise. They were to be allowed no access to the owner's bedroom, and indeed were not allowed up the stairs at all.

Case History – I'm the leader of the gang, I am

Recently I had to assist a breeder who was having pack order aggression problems among her Bearded Collies. She had a bitch who had reached thirteen months old and had decided she didn't have to be at the bottom of the pack any more, so she started working her way up by having a go at all of the lower-ranking bitches. In fact she one at a time took on every one of the bitches who offered any resistance, and won. Finally there was only the stud dog left, who was pack leader. His owners have always recognized this and encouraged all the others to do so as well. What usually happens when another dog is trying to work its way up to the top, especially when there are lots of dogs involved – as in this case where there were six – the ambitious, lowest-ranking one invariably starts gradually on one or two right at the bottom, and, once its fairly confident, just skips the rest and jumps straight to the top. And that's what she did. She just went straight after the male and started having fights and squabbles with him.

Unfortunately the owner did the worst thing possible by assuming that because these two weren't happy together, nor relating well, they should spend more time together, hoping they would become friends. Prior to all of this, the male had been the only one who was allowed to live indoors, so she brought in the female, thinking that if the two had more time with each other, they'd grow close. She started feeding them together, letting them both lie on the furniture and climb on her lap and so on. Of course, this created even more friction, because they then had still more opportunities to compete. She also started walking the dogs together. Not surprisingly, the aggression between the dogs increased. All these measures were just making things worse rather than better.

What had to be done was to change things and make it clear that the top dog was still the male. The bitch was then made second, making sure that all the rights that a second-in-command should have were established. She was always to be fed second, her lead put on second, she was allowed to get in and out of the car second, and so on. It was made very clear to her what the rules were and what the pack order was.

There was also a very different type of aggression being displayed by this bitch. She was bred for show, but had suddenly become aggressive toward judges in the ring when they tried to handle her. Although she had always tended to be a little fear-based, her aggression had escalated considerably when a physically handicapped judge had approached her in a shuffling manner of which she was clearly fearful, as it was something that she had not previously encountered. As he reached out to her, she went into a complete panic, and refused to let him near her. Of course, what made matters even worse was that the judge, rather than recognizing this and simply leaving the dog alone, kept going back and trying again and again to examine her, each time stressing the dog even more, and forcing the owner to keep trying to control her, telling her off and attempting to hold her still. All of these things added to the unpleasant associations that the dog was already beginning to form about being shown. Eventually the duo left the ring. From then on, the dog became hysterical whenever anyone tried to handle her, even people she knew well. By the time that the owner contacted me, she wouldn't even allow the husband to examine her. The only person that she would tolerate it from was the wife.

This demonstrates how much just a few interactions, or sometimes even one, can lead to a drastic change in a dog's behaviour, to the point of it using aggression to protect itself. In order to effect a cure, I recommended going back to basics in her training. Firstly, get one person she knows well, in this case the husband, to give the dog a few food treats, then, still holding treats in one hand, gently examine her head with the other, still offering her the food to help keep her mind off being handled. She would then be given even more food treats. This would teach her that there is something pleasant attached to being examined, and that the examination would not be long or too thorough before an even bigger reward was given. This procedure was repeated frequently, and the length of time she would be examined was gradually increased, moving slowly down the dog's body to cover other areas. They could then get someone else to repeat the procedure, then someone else, and so on. They could then try it at the training class, going right back to the beginning, having them start back at her head.

One of the first programmes I was asked to do was a case of pack order aggression. It involved two bitches – a German Shepherd and a small mongrel.

Case History – You and me against the world

The owner already had the mongrel when she found a female Shepherd as a stray. After she had reported her find to the relevant bodies, and no one had come forward to claim the dog, the woman decided to keep her. The mongrel bitch, who was much older, made it clear from the start that she was the boss, would tolerate no attempt at interaction by the Shepherd, and would attack her if she came too close or challenged her authority in any way. So the rank order was established and the two dogs co-existed in relative harmony.

A couple of years went by, and the owner was offered a third dog, a male German Shepherd cross. As things had gone so well between the two bitches, she accepted and took the dog home. He and the Shepherd bitch hit it off immediately, and became practically inseparable, much to the mongrel's annoyance. She seemed to like him even less than the other bitch, and would not have either of them anywhere near her.

Then one day, not long after the arrival of the male dog, a fight ensued between the two bitches. But this time things were different. On this occasion, instead of the usual scenario where the older mongrel had a go at the younger bitch, with her just trying to get clear of trouble as quickly as possible, it was the younger one who started the fight, approaching the older dog while she was resting and attacking her as soon as she looked up. The owner rushed in and separated them with no real damage done. However, this situation began to occur ever more frequently, invariably with the Shepherd bitch initiating the aggression, or simply intimidating the older dog to a point where she would growl a warning to the Shepherd, who would then immediately attack her, with increasing ferocity. The male dog showed no aggression in these situations, and never got involved in the fights. Finally, the fights became so frequent, and so intense, that the owner began to fear for the older dog's life, so she contacted me.

Before the arrival of the male dog, a clear hierarchy had been established. Both bitches had worked out the boundaries, and what each had to do in order to avoid a conflict. Despite the considerable difference in size, by her ferocity, the older dog had made it clear to the younger one that she was not going to be usurped in her own territory without a fight. The dog was not confident enough to challenge her and so things ticked along.

When the male dog arrived and formed an immediate bond with the young bitch, she felt that she had found an ally, and that with his help she could now overthrow the old dog. So she began to pick fights. The male dog never interjected, but that no longer mattered as she had realized she had a physical advantage over the older dog.

To cure the aggression, all we needed to do was to undermine the young bitch's confidence. To do this, we decided to form a new alliance between the male dog and the older bitch. The two dogs had no affinity towards each other and would never be friends, so the trick was to make it *appear* that they were. I told the owner to allow as little play between the two young dogs as possible. She was to walk the older bitch and the male dog together, to feed them together, to have them sleep upstairs together while the young bitch slept down-stairs. They would always be given treats together, while the young one had to wait until they had finished.

The result was that the young bitch now felt that the male had transferred his allegiance to the older bitch, and she was not confident enough to challenge both of them, so the aggression stopped.

In summary:

1   Make sure that your dog knows that, however much you love it, its place in the pack will always be below your family and anyone else you invite into your home. That way you should avoid it challenging those it shouldn't.

2   If you have more than one dog, and one is clearly trying to dominate the other, decide which dog you want to be dominant and promote that dog heavily, making sure that it gets *everything* first. Sometimes this can be morally quite difficult for the owner to do, as it is often the newest dog that is asserting itself, and the owner is then faced with demoting the old dog that they may have had for many years. But it will be the quickest way to end conflict between the dogs, and so in the long run will be in the older dog's interest too.

3   In some cases you may find that castrating the lower ranked of two male dogs will help speed up the process if the dogs are of the same sex. If you have two bitches, you should spay the most dominant of the two. This removes the bulk of her female hormones, making her more domi-nant still, and increasing the distance between the two bitches. If there is only one dog, castration may help if he is being aggressive towards a member or members of the 'human pack'.

Chase/predatory Aggression

This is possibly the hardest type of aggression to eliminate. It can be focused at a number of different targets, depending upon what each individual dog considers to be its 'prey'. Sometimes it is specific, with the dog only chasing one particular stimulus, such as squirrels. It can also involve many others, and I have known of more than one dog that will chase anything that moves quickly – cats, cars, joggers, children, rabbits, sheep, bicycles, and even the sun reflecting off of a watch face. Collie-type dogs often display these behaviours, as they were selectively bred to chase and bite at the heels of what they considered to be prey animals. It is frequently seen in dogs of this type that may never have seen a 'prey animal' in their lives. Go to throw a ball for most Border Collies and they will immediately assume a predatory body posture.

Case History – A-hunting we will go . . .

A Golden Retriever I met recently displayed predatory behaviour to the extreme, but only with one type of prey – squirrels. His owner would take him to the local park, which was very large, with several densely wooded areas, and let him off the lead. Immediately he would streak to the nearest of these areas, often not even bothering to do the customary scent-marking so important to most young male dogs. Away he would go, with never a backward glance, going from one wooded section to another, rarely if ever looking for his owner. Frequently she would lose him altogether, and would wander the park sometimes for hours until she would spot him somewhere, still looking for more squirrels, apparently unaware of having misplaced his owner at all. His owner would shout and scream at him, all to no avail. He carried on oblivious, only stopping if she managed to get close enough to intimidate him into waiting for her to catch him up, put the lead on and take him home.

A dog that has taken his predatory behaviour to this extreme is very difficult to cure reliably. So in order to change his behaviour you need to find a way of employing that predatory drive, rather than trying to extinguish it. Teach the dog to become obsessed with a particular toy, one that is never left around for the dog to play with whenever it likes, and then get bored with. This toy will only be used by you to play with him, and as soon as you finish playing, put the toy away again. Always play *with* the dog, rather than let him play by himself. This way you become much more fun and exciting to the dog. Play lots of tugging games with the dog, always ensuring that you end up with the toy, not the dog. That way he learns that you are in control, and that if he wants to play the best game, he has to come to you. If your dog is one of those who, having got hold of the toy, will not let go, regardless of how many times you tell him to, place a taste deterrent on a finger of the opposite hand from the one holding the toy before you begin playing. Oil of clove often works well, and you can buy this at a chemist. When you are ready to end the game, tell the dog to 'LEAVE'. If he refuses, simply stick the finger with the deterrent under his lip. Once he gets a taste, he should let go. If that fails, you could use a sound deterrent, described below. Practising calling him several times a day for a favourite treat or game will teach him to come back more reliably too, giving greater control even when he has seen a prey animal. Hopefully, the dog should start to find this game as rewarding as chasing the squirrels, especially as he knows that he will get the toy at the end, something that he probably fails to do when chasing prey animals.

However, sometimes the dog finds chasing the prey animal more important and rewarding than anything that the owner can offer. In this case the owner needs to attach a consequence to the dog choosing the wrong reward. For this I recommend a **sound deterrent**. A can with pebbles in it, an old bunch of keys or an old check chain all work well: the point is to use something that rattles. The owner should get hold of a few soft drinks cans, put a few pebbles or screws into each and stick some sticky tape over the hole. Dot lots of these all around the house. If the dog is given a command and he ignores it, the owner should pick up a tin and repeat the command. If the dog still refuses to obey, the owner should throw the tin in his direction, *not so it hits him,* but so that it lands fairly close to him, close enough for him to think that it was intended to hit him. As the tin is thrown, they should repeat the command in exactly the same tone of voice, so he learns to respond without being shouted at. Chances are he will stop doing whatever he shouldn't have been doing. He will then learn to associate that sound with the owner's ability to punish him from a distance without having to chase him. The owner could obviously substitute chains or keys for the cans.

Although this method can work very well, it does mean a great deal of work on the owner's part at gaining a much greater level of control over the dog than they perhaps had previously.

To help avoid your dog developing this problem, think ahead. If you allow your dog to chase some animals, there is a real possibility that it will learn to chase others. For example, many owners allow their dog to chase squirrels because they think that the dog will never catch one. The first problem with this is that the dog is all the time developing a desire to chase that will get stronger and stronger the longer it is allowed to carry out this behaviour. Secondly, the dog is likely to move on to chasing other animals such as cats and rabbits. Maybe even sheep, if you ever take the dog to a place that has them. Suddenly, when faced with the prospect of your dog being shot for worrying sheep, you realize that you have a problem. But it is a problem that you initially encouraged. Who is at fault, the dog or the owner?

14   Excessive Attention-seeking

Attention-seeking behaviour can sometimes be amusing, especially in the presence of guests. Cécile recounts an unusual example of this type of behaviour from her own dogs. Both of her Great Danes have had a habit which is expertly practised by this breed, as their size and long legs make it easy for them. The trick is to stand in front of their quarry facing away from them, then very slowly, and almost imperceptibly, back up toward them until quite suddenly the victim finds some sixty kilograms or more of dog sitting in their lap! Usually this produces roars of laughter, especially when it happens for the first time and the person is caught totally unawares. Of course, to avoid the risk of it happening to someone frail, elderly or very small like a child, she tried to discourage it at all times.

Her Danes also had an infallible method of stopping her from working at her desk or easel. It would begin with the dog just sitting innocently beside her. Then a heavy paw is rested on her lap. If she ignored it and carried on working, both paws would be placed there. Eventually the dog's entire front half would be resting on her lap. All she could see was a very large head between her and her work! I advised her that this should *never* be tolerated, as it could lead to quite unacceptable behaviour later on.

Attention-seeking is one of the many ways in which dogs try to communicate with other dogs and people. In some cases, the dog will often simply be trying to obtain something it considers vital to its well-being – food or water, or perhaps to be allowed out to relieve itself. Some dogs however will use gaining attention primarily as a means of reassuring themselves of their ability to control their owners. It is imperative that the owner control the behaviour of these dogs, if serious problems are to be avoided.

A dog that is successful in controlling too much of the owner's behaviour will frequently become very difficult to train, as, rather than learning, it is far too busy training its owners. For this dog to be responsive to its owners demands, it would have to relinquish a lot of the control it has worked so hard to acquire. Dogs are not usually very keen to do that. Training their owners takes many different forms, some are obvious to the owners, some less so, and it is usually very time-consuming for a dog. If you have an attention-seeking dog, you may be able to relate to the following case histories.

Case History – Who's been sitting in my chair?

An owner rang me to arrange to have her dog neutered through the animal welfare department. As I conversed with her, I could hear what sounded like growling in the background. I asked her if that was the dog that I could hear, and she replied that it was indeed her dog growling at her, warning her to pay attention to it. The dog was a 9-month-old Cavalier King Charles Spaniel. I asked her why it was growling, and she said it was because she was sitting in his chair. With that, she let out a yelp. I asked her what had happened, and she said that the dog had just bitten her for not giving up the chair. I advised her that she should seriously consider dealing with this problem, but she was adamant that it would rectify itself as the dog got older. I tried to explain that it doesn't work that way, but she was insistent. Three months later, she rang me back to ask if we would take the dog, as it was now viciously attacking her if she did anything it didn't like, almost always drawing blood.

An interesting thing about the way that dogs train their owners is that they are much less direct in their early training of us than we are of them, so often we do not realize that we are being trained at all. In one day, try to count how many times your dog forces an interaction from you, or tries to make you respond to something it is doing. Observe how readily you react to the dog, stroking it whenever it tells you to, letting it out every time that it demands it, even though it only went out a short while ago. And how difficult you find it to refuse the dog, or if you do refuse, how guilty it makes you feel. How many times does it bring you a toy and command you to throw it, refusing to take no for an answer? How many times does it bark at nothing, knowing that you will stop what you are doing and tell it to be quiet, or come to investigate?

Having counted up all of those attempted moments of gaining attention, observe how many times you try to control the dog in an average day, and your success rate. You may well find that you:

a) Try to gain attention from him far fewer times than he does from you;

b) You are far less successful than he is at actually getting what you want on the first command if you are not offering a reward; and

c) Frequently, the best you will get from him will be a compromise, where he will do some of what you asked him, but only to a degree.

The reason for this is simple. By proving time and again that he is able to control you, in his mind he assures himself of a high status within the pack – equal to, or perhaps even higher than yours. If he were then suddenly to become responsive to your commands, he would be relinquishing that control, and all of his hard work would have been for nothing. Obviously he would be reluctant to do this.

Case History – It's *bad* to talk

Another example of a dog trying desperately to control its owner through attention-seeking occurred with a 3-year-old male English Bull Terrier I was asked to visit. The owner had pandered to the dog ever since she had acquired it from the rescue kennels. This is a common mistake new owners of rescue dogs often make, believing that they should over-compensate for whatever they think that the dog has suffered in a previous home. Anyway, the result was that the dog completely controlled the owner. It had realized that when the phone rang, the owner would pay it little if any attention, and it was not prepared to accept that. So it devised a very effective method of control. As soon as the phone rang, the dog would run to the table on which the phone sat, and pull the cable, yanking the phone off the table. It would then sit on the phone, snarling at the owner, refusing to let her anywhere near it. If you have ever encountered a snarling English Bull Terrier, you will know them to be a pretty effective deterrent, and the owner would invariably let discretion prove the better part of valour, thereby rewarding that behaviour.

Basically, what all owners of dogs should try to do is ensure that they never help to create a situation that at some point in the future they will find unacceptable. It may be fine to let your puppy bite your hands when you are not paying it attention, but will you still be happy to let your adult dog bite your hands? If not, don't allow it to bite when it is a puppy.

Case History – How a Staffordshire lost his tail

Some owners realize too late that letting their dog learn a particular attention-seeking behaviour can be not only a nuisance, but can also have disastrous consequences for both the dog and the owner later on, as the dog often takes the behaviour too far. An example of this was a Staffordshire Bull Terrier who started chasing his tail. Bull Terriers are notorious clowns and love to entertain, and when he first started to do this, everyone would stop what they were doing to laugh at him. The result was that the dog learned that this was a very good way to get attention.

After a while though, the novelty of this game wore off and the family ceased to be amused by it, and would invariably ignore the dog when it did this. The dog couldn't understand why it no longer got laughed at anymore, so did what it thought had worked previously in getting it noticed. It stepped up the pace of the chasing. Faster and faster it went, but still no one seemed to notice. Then one day, the dog actually caught the end of its tail and bit it, holding on tenaciously. The family gasped and stopped to acknowledge this new behaviour, and the die was cast. The dog now came to believe that the new way to be noticed was to bite the end of its tail.

And this it did – and the less notice people took, the harder the dog worked.

Finally the dog actually succeeded in biting the end of its tail off, splashing blood everywhere. This gained it immediate attention, but it had now definitely stopped being funny. As far as the dog was concerned, it would now have to work even harder to catch its tail as it was shorter. The stump of its tail began to show damage, and when the family spoke to the vet, he advised them that they should have the terminal vertebrae amputated to stop any further damage. Reluctantly, they agreed. Unfortunately, the dog had now become obsessed with tail-chasing, especially as the end of its tail was now painful, and would do it even if the owners were not present. They came home one day to find the room blood-spattered again. More vertebrae were removed. Same result. In the end, the vet removed the dog's tail altogether, and that finally stopped the behaviour. All this was the result of letting the dog make its owners respond to its demands for attention, and them not recognizing the dangers.

Puppies often learn that a very good way of gaining attention is to do something that they know that they shouldn't. Picture this scenario. An owner has a 9-week-old puppy. It hasn't had its vaccinations yet, so the owner cannot take the puppy to the park to burn off some energy playing with other dogs yet. The owner sits at home watching the television. The puppy is bored. It throws around one of its toys for a while, but soon loses interest in it. It tries to get a response from the owner, but he is far too occupied in his favourite soap opera, and continues to ignore the pup. Finally he decides to chew something different – the edge of the sofa. After a minute or two, the owner notices how quiet the dog has been, so looks to see what it is up to, and discovers it playing tug-of-war with the sofa cover. The owner leaps up, gives the puppy a firm 'NO' command, and proceeds to distract the puppy, entertaining it with one of its toys, hoping that the puppy will focus on that instead. Unfortunately, what the dog starts to learn is that the best way to get attention from you when you won't pay it any is to chew something that it is not supposed to.

Sometimes we see really bizarre attention-seeking behaviours, such as chasing invisible flies, barking at invisible intruders and even deliberate self-mutilation, and most of these behaviours will have been caused by the attention it received for doing these things originally. However, these things have a way of becoming obsessive, and should not be encouraged.

Case History – I'll name that tune in one!

Another case of attention-seeking occurred with a young Border Collie cross. The owner absolutely adored the dog, and gave in to every demand it made. It had taught the owner to entertain it almost constantly. If she were reading, she would have to be stroking the dog at the same time. If she were eating, she would have to share the food with the dog. The owner had a passion for soap operas, and the dog had learned that whenever it heard certain theme tunes, the owner would pay it no attention. So at the first few bars of her favourite soap opera, the dog would run off into the kitchen and bring back one of its toys. The owner would then be expected to throw the toy for the duration of the programme. When the dog heard the tune a second time, it would lose interest in the game as it knew that it no longer needed to compete against the television for the owner's attention.

This illustrates the learning ability of a dog in a situation that it finds unacceptable, and its ability to re-train its owners to behave in a way that reinstates its control over them.

So start as you mean to go on, never letting your dog control you. Whether it realizes it or not, this will in the long run benefit neither of you. Throughout the day, try not to let your dog force you to pay it attention. If it tries to gain attention by chasing its tail, or pacing up and down in front of you, or nudging your hand to make you stroke it, or whining or barking, or staring at you trying to make you look back at it, *completely ignore it*. Don't even tell it to stop what it is doing, as this will still be giving it attention by acknowledging what it is doing. Instead, simply ignore it, get up and move away from it, or leave the room. It will soon learn that it cannot control you. You can still do all of the above things, such as stroking it or playing with it, just never when the dog tries to make you do them. Sticking to this attitude helps teach the dog that you are in control of what the pack does and when, and will therefore help in other aspects of the dog's training.

15 Separation Anxieties (Dogs That Can't Bear Being Alone)

Years before she had ever heard of me, Cécile was in a most distressing situation with her first Great Dane, one that she hadn't anitcipated, and found herself at a loss to control.

She and her husband had adopted him from the breed's rescue centre when he was eleven months old, and four weeks later, her husband died. For the first time, she had to go out and leave the dog on its own. Cécile was not yet out of earshot when he started howling like the 'Hound of the Baskervilles': a low, mournful 'Oh woe, wooooe', increasing in volume until the sound wafted far across the green behind the garden. Besides being overcome with grief, she was frantic, desperately sorry for the dog, and fearful that neighbours would complain.

As they had only lived in the area for two months and didn't really know anyone very well, the local residents' association put an advert in their newsletter on her behalf advertising for a baby-sitter for the dog. It was spotted by a local newspaper, who found it so amusing they featured an article about them with a photo, which in turn was taken up by Thames Television who came out and filmed them in an interview for the evening news programme. The results were mixed, some hilarious, some disastrous, but in the end, some very kind neighbours did volunteer and Cécile made some wonderful friends as well as finding sitters.

Of course as time went on, there were days when she had to leave her Dane on his own. She frequently returned home to find rubbish wall to wall, from overturned dustbin and waste paper baskets, the refrigerator, and upper as well as lower kitchen cupboards, raided by a dog over two metres in height on his hind legs. This necessitated the tying up of door handles and the installation of a child-proof refrigerator lock from Mothercare. He could open *any* door, using either teeth, nose or paws, so it took a good half an hour to secure everything every time she left the house.

Separation anxieties and fear-based aggression are the two most common behaviours that I am asked to look at. In cases of separation anxiety, you have a dog that for a number of possible reasons, listed below, has reached a stage where it cannot cope with being left by its owner or owners.

The nail-chewer

Like a person who chews their nails in stressful situations, this dog wants something to chew on to take its mind off the anxiety it is feeling.

Given an option, he will usually choose personal items that smell strongly of the owners. Favourite choices are socks, shoes and underwear, as these are usually heavily impregnated with the owner's scent. Anything this dog gets hold of will usually not only be chewed, it will be completely destroyed – torn into tiny pieces. If he chooses impersonal items, he tends to chew a little out of a lot of things, rather than focusing on just one item. Impersonal destruction tends to be centred on the last place that the dog saw the owner, so the door may be clawed, the carpet by the front door pulled up and so on.

The giver of unwanted gifts

He's the one who leaves little (or maybe not so little) presents for you to dispose of on your return. He tends to foul in a number of places, rather than just one, as the stress of being left repeatedly loosens his bowel and bladder control. If he defecates, it's usually diarrhoea, again because of the stress he's under. Why, however, do they always choose the expensive carpet, or the oriental rug to do it on, instead of the lino in the kitchen?

The blues singer

This is the dog that can invariably be heard howling as though it carries the weight of the world on her shoulders. It wants to let everyone know how it is feeling, and calls tirelessly for those it has lost. And just like its namesake, everyone soon tires of hearing her and want her to shut up as no one's interested in what it has to say.

The centre of attention

This dog craves almost constant attention. It will insist on being entertained, and will pester you to let him be the centre of your world, turning up when you least want him to, every time that you try to do something that doesn't involve him. But the fact that he succeeds in gaining your attention assures him of his ability to control you, which will inevitably make him worse.

I usually find that when I speak to the owners of these dogs, they say that the dog follows them everywhere while they are at home, and this is where the problem usually begins. While the owner is at home, the dog insists on having *constant* access to them. It usually sleeps in the owner's bedroom, often on the bed, and naps on their feet while they are anywhere downstairs, if it is not lying beside them on the sofa. It sits watching them while they are in the bathroom, or whimpers outside the door if the owner shuts it out of the room. If the owner has gone out without the dog, even if it is just for two minutes, the dog will act as though it hasn't seen them for years when they return, leaping like a jack-rabbit and doing the 'Wall of Death' around the hallway. The owner who allows their dog to do these things is almost certain to end up with a dog that is so over-bonded with them that it cannot entertain or occupy itself. It constantly demands attention, and will often go to extraordinary lengths to get it.

Case History - Brothers in arms

Here is another example of the type of destruction that can be caused by a dog with a separation anxiety. I was contacted by the owner of a Labrador bitch. Among the problems her owner had with her was a rather more extreme behaviour.

Whenever the owner tried to separate herself from the dog, it panicked and scratched furiously at the door to get out. So, in an effort to stop the dog doing any damage, the owner would rush back in and scold it. Unfortunately, what the dog had learnt was that scratching was a good way to get the owner to come back to it. It didn't mind the punishment – it was worth it to get back to her owner. To minimize the damage that the dog could cause when left, the owner would leave the dog locked in the bathroom. The dog would begin to scratch at the door as soon as the owner left it. But however hard it tried, it couldn't scratch its way through. So it moved to the wall next to the door, and found that its claws could cause significant damage to the wall. By the time the owner came home, there was the dog sitting in the hallway by the front door looking very pleased with herself, after having created a Labrador-sized walkway through from the bathroom to the hall without ever having to use the door.

How to tell if your dog suffers from separation anxiety

If you have a dog that is destructive when left, take a look at this questionnaire. It may help you decide if the destruction that your dog has caused is related to a separation anxiety, or is due to some other problem. Choose the answer that best applies to your dog. If one particular question does not apply to your dog, leave it and go on to the next one.

1 Does your dog tend to chew the same type of thing, or a variety of things?
   a The same type of things.
   b A variety of things.

2 What type of things is he more likely to chew given the opportunity?
    a Carpets, furniture, plants etc: impersonal items.
    b Clothes, shoes, handbags etc: personal items.

3 If he chews personal items, do they belong to one particular person?
    a No.
    b Yes.

4 If he chews non-personal items, is the destruction aimed at doors and windows?
    a No.
    b Yes.

5 Is he only destructive when left on his own?
    a Sometimes when people are present.
    b Only when he is alone.

6 Is he happy to be separated from you in every room with the door closed?
    a Yes.
    b No.

7 If the destruction is accompanied by messing and urinating, is there just one spot or many?
    a One.
    b Many.

8 Would your dog be more likely to chew when left for:
    a More than half an hour, or
    b Less than half an hour?

9 Is he *always* destructive when left by himself:
    a No.
    b Yes.

10 When you return, does the dog:
    a Avoid you, or
    b Greet you?

11 If the dog greets you after destruction has occurred, does
   he seem:
    a Very excited and happy to see you, or
    b Stressed, anxious, and over-attached to you for some
    time afterwards.

Now look over your answers. You should see a pattern. If you have more 'a' answers, then the problem is unlikely to be stress-related, and may be a result of boredom or attention-seeking. If you have more 'b' answers the behaviour is probably stress-related, due to a separation anxiety.

Case History – When I'm calling you-ooo-ooo

An owner contacted me because she had received complaints from neighbours about her dog barking when left. When I visited her, I was amazed at the lengths she went to in order to comfort it, and to assure it of her intention to return as quickly as possible. Firstly the dog had come to recognize things she saw her owner doing as meaning she would soon be leaving. As soon as the owner used her hair-spray, the dog began to show signs of stress. At that point the owner would begin reassuring the dog verbally. 'It's all right darling, Mummy's not going for a while yet.'

Each thing that the owner did after that, or indeed almost any movement that she made after that would result in more stress for the dog, and more 'reassurance' from the owner. 'I really hate leaving you baby, but I have to so I can afford to feed you.'

Finally, after maybe fifteen minutes of this, the dog would be very, very stressed. The owner then calls the dog to her, picks her up and places her in her own bed, not the dog's, which lies next to hers. Not content with placing the dog on the bed, she puts the dog under the duvet and tucks her in, talking reassuringly to her all the time, apologizing for having to leave her once again. She then takes a few dog biscuits and lays them on the pillow, next to the dog's head. Lastly, she would take the bedside clock, show the dog the current position of the hands, then show the dog the position the hands would be in when she was due to return, telling the dog 'You see the long hand is on the twelve and the short hand is on the eight. When the short hand goes round to the eleven, Mummy will be back.' Then, overflowing with guilt, she mournfully leaves the house.

By the time that the owner actually went out the door, she had caused the dog so much stress that it would have been a miracle if the dog had not developed some form of separation anxiety. When I interviewed the owner further, I found that the dog was very controlling of the owner when she was at home, and constantly demanded attention, which the owner felt obliged to give her as she still felt guilty for having left her.

If the dog heard the theme tune for the owner's favourite soap opera, she would run and get her ball and force the owner to throw it continually for the entire programme. As soon as she heard the tune a second time, she would drop the ball, uninterested. The same was true of any other programme that the owner watched on a regular basis. This was because the dog had learned that these were times that the owner would pay her no attention, and she would not allow this.

Let's look at how this behaviour can actually begin. Usually if you arrive home to find that the dog has been destructive, you will punish it. There are several reasons why this may actually make the problem worse rather than better.

Let us suppose that you leave the house at 8 a.m. The dog gets stressed when you leave it, and, knowing your routine, it actually starts to get stressed at 7.25 a.m. So for thirty-five minutes the dog's stress level steadily increases, until at 7.55 a.m. you start saying goodbye to the dog. Through watching previous 'leaving rituals', such as putting on your coat and hat, the dog now knows that you are about to leave him all by himself. Now the stress level goes through the roof. Then suddenly, he is alone. He runs into the living-room and watches you go down the path, he hears the car starting up and sees you driving away, and he knows he will not see you again for a very long time. He whines or howls for a time, perhaps even barks a little, but to no avail. So he looks for a way to relieve all the stress he is now feeling. He starts to scratch at the carpet by the front door, tentatively at first, then with more vigour, but still you do not return. He jumps up at the door, scratching the paint. Still no sign of you. He runs into the living-room and looks out of the window, but his claw catches in the curtain and he tears it. Once he frees himself he goes back to lying by the front door, sighing softly.

At 6.15 p.m. you return home to find that you cannot get the front door open. You really put your back into it, and finally get it open far enough to squeeze your way in. The dog is leaping up at you, thrilled that you have come home, but you are furious. The dog looks up at you and sees your angry face. He knows that that face means he is about to be punished, but as he committed the damage more than ten hours earlier he has *no* idea what he is going to be punished for. He tries to slink away, but you call him back and point to the raised and torn carpet. He still does not relate the carpet to himself when you lash out at him, hitting him on the side of the head. He tries to run away but you call him back, grab him by the collar, point to the carpet once again yelling, 'BAD DOG', and push his nose to the carpet shouting, 'NO'. You throw him away from you in disgust. Then you go into the living-room to try to relax, and see the torn curtain. You call the dog into the living-room and shut the door behind him, rolling your sleeves up, and reaching for yesterday's newspaper.

The next day you get up and repeat the whole process of getting ready for work. The dog does all the things that it did the day before because it is still stressed, and when you come home you also do the same thing as the day before as you are also stressed.

On day three, you decide to lock the living-room door to stop the dog tearing the curtains. Now he cannot even watch you leave. Added to this is the fact that, although he cannot remember why, he is now beginning to associate your leaving him with something very unpleasant. He is even more stressed. This time you come home to find all the previous destruction in the hall, but you also notice that he has clawed at the living-room door, badly damaging the paint, and has messed and urinated as well. The dog has begun to realize that when things are not where they should be he gets punished. The trouble is, he cannot remember how they got messed up in the first place. So you rub his nose in the faeces and urine again using the 'BAD DOG!' and 'NO!' verbal punishments, and drag him into the living-room to get the newspaper you fortunately left in there yesterday. If a dog is stressed about you leaving him, using aggression on him for the destruction will probably only increase the stress, thereby increasing the likelihood of destruction. You should therefore try to decrease the stress.

If your dog has a separation anxiety, there are lots of things that you can do to control it, or even eliminate it completely. Firstly, as your dog is using gaining attention as a means of convincing itself that it can control you and your movements, you need to ensure that you ignore every attempt by your dog to gain attention, unless it relates to the dog needing to go out to relieve itself. Sometimes though, dogs will use even this to gain attention. So if your dog asks to go out twenty times a day, or five minutes after it has just been, chances are it is just trying to control you.

You can still give him as much attention as you want, just never when he tries to initiate it. By ignoring him I mean not touching him, speaking to him or even looking at him, as all of these things reward him with a response, which is exactly what he wanted.

For the same reason, you should not play with him when he tells you to. This is another way in which he can control you, and the more in control he is, the less in control you are. Again, you can still play with him as often as you wish, just never when he gives you something and *orders* you to. You may already have noticed how often he wants to play when you are doing something that doesn't involve him – watching television or talking on the phone.

Try not to let him follow you all around the house. If you cannot get your dog to accept being separate from you while you are still in the house, what chance have you got of him accepting you going out? To do this you can erect a baby gate or put a clothes-horse across a doorway and leave him in another room. They can often accept this much better than you closing the door in their face. Then you can gradually close the door, a couple of inches at a time over a number of days. Keep alternating the rooms that he is left in so that he learns to be left in different environments.

While he is separated from you give him a favourite chew

to focus on. This helps him to think of being separated as potentially rewarding, as you attach a positive association to being left. When you return to him, take it away again, so that he learns to focus on it, as he knows that you might come and take it away at any moment. For the time that he is separated from you, it is very important that you ignore him *completely*. If you are continually paying him attention while he is in another room, you will not be preparing him for real separation, when he will get no attention at all.

If he sleeps in your bedroom, it is important that you remove him from the room at night, perhaps giving him a bed in the hallway outside the bedroom door. This will separate him from you for about a third of his day, but as you are still in the house, and you will both be asleep for most of that time, he should be able to cope with this. If you are worried that he will howl if you shut him out, try using the baby gate so he can still see you.

What happens if we use the same treatment for a dog that is destructive out of boredom? As a puppy, the dog learned that if he was bored and chewed something that he should not, you would give him attention and play with him with his own toys. So now that he is older, and you have just left for work at 8 a.m. he plods around looking for something to do, and remembers that chewing the wrong things always gets you to come and play with him. So he starts with the carpet, pulling it up from the corner and ripping up the underlay. After doing this for a while he stops and waits for you to come and tell him off, as most dogs prefer the attention of being punished to no attention at all. You do not reappear. So he moves on to your favourite armchair. He pulls the cushion off and sets to work destroying it. When he is satisfied that it is really dead, he steps back and waits for you to rush in, scolding him. Nothing. So on he goes, all the time believing that soon you will come back, tell him off and then play with him.

Finally, at 6.15 p.m., you arrive home, only to find that you cannot get the front door open. When after some considerable effort you manage to get it open, you find that the carpet is torn to shreds, and that the dog obviously tried eating some of the underlay, but his digestive system rejected it so he threw it up all over the place, including onto the piece of floor on which you are standing, and you can feel it seeping into the hole in your shoe. Needless to say, the dog is nowhere to be seen. You enter the living-room to find that the sofa and armchair are both devoid of cushions, but that the stuffing from them is everywhere. The telephone cable has been chewed through, as has the cable for the standard lamp. More vomit. More ripped carpet. The bin has been emptied all over the floor and you can just make out the chewed remnants of a rolled-up newspaper, urinated on of course. And there, in the corner, is the cause of all your pain, standing on the arm of the surviving armchair, cooling his dry throat, having a refreshing guzzle from the goldfish bowl. He realizes that you are there and seems to melt off of the chair and pour his way over to your feet, looking terribly guilty, but believing that finally you have come to play with him. Fear of killing him prevents you making physical contact, so you leave the room and go upstairs, saying nothing.

An hour later, when you have calmed down, you return to find him lying sadly by the wrecked armchair. You quietly tell him he is a bad dog and begin cleaning up. The next day all the behaviours of the previous day are repeated by both parties, only this time you grab hold of him and shake him, screaming obscenities, vowing to get rid of him if he does it again.

Two days later we find him sitting in a kennel at the local rescue centre.

If a dog is bored try gradually to increase the lengths of time that he is left on his own, while providing a stimulus such as a raw marrow-bone. When the marrow inside has been licked out you can refill it with a tasty treat such as cream-cheese or fish paste. *You must always remove this immediately on your return* and the dog must not have constant access either to this bone or any others. To prevent a new puppy becoming destructive, if possible, leave it only for very short periods of time during the day until the dog gets used to it, and increase these so gradually that the puppy can always cope without worrying. During the times that the puppy must be left for longer periods, during the night for example, put him in a kennel if he is still being destructive. Most good pet shops sell them, and although they may seem expensive, they are a lot cheaper than replacing damaged furniture, and you can always sell it on after you have finished using it. If you still find that too expensive you could try using a second-hand babies' play-pen with steel bars.

If you own a dog, particularly a puppy or a young dog that doesn't have this problem, you can still practise doing these things to ensure that he never develops it. You will also find that dogs that are less in control of their owners are generally easier to train, as they are less busy training *you*.

16 Excessive/Inappropriate Barking

Almost everyone who owns a dog wants them to bark or make some sort of noise in some situations. The problem arises when the dog starts barking and continues – indefinitely! The trouble is we sometimes encourage them to bark: at the door; at anyone approaching who seems strange; or to keep cats or other animals out of our gardens.

Before you can cure the barking, you need to be able to tell why he is barking in the first place. Perhaps he is barking because he has been left alone, or is bored. Or maybe he is anxious about being left, and this is what is causing him to bark. Or it could be that he is barking as a means of gaining attention.

Whatever his reason for barking, he has obviously convinced himself that this is an appropriate behaviour, and will get him what he wants. Your job is to convince him that this is no longer necessary, or that it no longer works.

Recognizing the boredom barker

A dog barking out of boredom will usually start barking some time after the owners leave the house, once he is fed up with playing with his toys, digging up the garden, exploring the house and so on. The barking is usually pretty continuous. There may also be some destruction with this dog, and the things that are chewed appear to be random, clothes, books, furniture, house plants and the like. The things that have been chewed will usually only have been damaged, as the dog will have become bored with them as well, and will have probably moved on to something else. This is the type of dog that stands in the middle of the room barking at nothing in particular.

This type of dog is usually quite independent even while its owners are at home. It will often be off on its own, getting up to some form of mischief in another part of the house.

Quieting the boredom barker

One thing that people often try is leaving toys down constantly to keep the dog occupied. What quickly happens is that the dog becomes bored with the toys as he has constant access to them, so he looks elsewhere for entertainment, and will invariably choose the things that you don't want him to.

Remove all toys and bones that are lying around the house. Buy one fresh marrow-bone from the butcher's. When you go out, and the dog is left at home alone, leave the bone down for the dog to chew. Return after about fifteen minutes, by which time the dog should have just started to get stuck into the bone in earnest. When you return, take the bone away from him *immediately*. He must be encouraged to believe that if he doesn't make the most of the bone straightaway, you will come home and take it from him. This will encourage him to focus on it rather than on chewing anything else, and should distract him sufficiently to break the cycle of him barking. When he has stripped the bone of meat and marrow, rather than throwing it away, you can line the inside of the bone with something even tastier like soft cheese or fish paste. The dog will spend ages trying to get it out of all of the cracks. As the dog learns to spend more time on the bone, you can gradually increase the time that the dog is left. Alternatively, you can use a 'Kong toy' filled in the same way, or one of the activity toys that release small amounts of food as the dog rolls them around the floor.

Recognizing the anxious barker

This dog will usually start to bark very soon after the owner leaves the house, sometimes as soon as the owner is out of sight or earshot, and otherwise within five to ten minutes. He will normally bark in bursts, stopping to hear if the owner has heard his cries and is returning to him. This dog will not play with toys that are left down to amuse it. This dog usually follows its owner everywhere while they are at home, even if they are just going to the toilet or crossing the room. There is often destruction caused by this dog also. However, this dog's destruction is far from random. It will be centred around exits such as doors and windows, particularly the door that it last saw the owner go through. Perhaps the carpet by the front door has been pulled up and chewed. If property has been chewed it will tend to be personal things like clothing, shoes, socks and underwear, things that smell strongly of the owner. It will often favour the clothing of a particular person.

Quieting the anxious barker

Again, it is no good leaving toys down for this dog, as he will show no interest. It is too stressed to be interested in playing by itself. To alleviate the problem, you have to teach the dog that it is no longer the centre of attention. The dog must accept you doing things on your own terms, rather than him influencing your actions.

It is essential that the dog loses its ability to control your actions. This it does by making you respond to demands for attention. So you must whenever possible ignore all the dog's attempts to make you respond to things that he does: for example, bringing you a ball to throw; sitting in front of you, staring at you; muzzling your arm to make you stroke him; or jumping all over you when you return home. All of these things are examples of ways in which a dog perfects his skill at making you obedient. Once he is convinced that he has that control, he will use that power to try and make you do other things, such as coming when he calls you. If he does try any of these things you should not respond in any way, indeed you should not even look at him, as even this is a response that the dog will notice. You can still play with him, stroke him and do all of the things that you currently do to interact with him, just never when he initiates it. So when you are ready, call him over to you and *you* start the interaction. Similarly, it must be you that ends the interaction. If the dog tries to get you to keep doing something after you have stopped, it is vital that he should fail to make you do so.

The vast majority of owners who have a dog with this problem say that they cannot leave the dog separated from them, even while they are still in the house. If they go into another room, the dog insists on going too. With some, the dog will not even let them cross the room. If the owner sits down, the dog will lie beside them, making sure that a part of him is in constant contact with his owner, so that they cannot go anywhere without him knowing. It is imperative that this obsessive over-bonding be broken if the owner is to succeed in re-educating the dog, as if he will not accept being separated from his owner while they are still in the house, how will he ever accept them leaving?

So you start off by separating yourself from the dog, one room at a time. The most important room to separate this type of dog from is the bedroom. The average person spends a third of their life in that room, so by removing your dog from the bedroom anytime that you are in there, you will straight away be teaching him to accept separation for that length of time. This separation must mean that he is not allowed into the bedrooms *at all*. So no more leaving the door open with you chasing him out every ten minutes. If necessary put up a baby gate or a clothes horse across the door to keep him out, if you feel that you cannot close the door completely, or you feel that he may cry and disturb you or your neighbours. While he is separated from you, you can give him the bone to occupy him, but again, remember to remove it as soon as you return to him.

While you are moving around the house during the day, continue to separate him from you in different rooms. When you do this, say nothing to him that advertises that you are leaving the room, as these things in themselves will only increase his stress. Simply get up and leave the room. If the dog manages to get out of the room before you, call him back in and start again. If the dog goes completely mad when you return, jumping around and whining and barking as though you have been gone for a week instead of five minutes, continue to ignore him until he is behaving in a calm manner. Then give him a little bit of fuss. If he gets over-excited at this, go back to ignoring him.

Some people find that it helps to leave a radio on. This only seems to help if the owner usually has a radio on while they are at home normally. If they do not, the dog will not find the radio comforting as he will make no association between the radio playing and his owners. You can also try leaving an item of your clothing outside the door that has your scent on it, so that he can smell something familiar just outside.

Recognizing the attention-seeking barker

This barking is often worst of all when the owner is present, but not paying any attention to the dog. For example, when the phone rings, the dog may jump up barking and dashing around. It realizes that once the owner gets on the phone, they will pay him no attention, and he is not happy about this. So he objects – very loudly! This dog will often choose these moments to try to make the owner play with it. So perhaps it will run off and get a toy, and make the owner throw it all the time that they are on the phone. Then as soon as the owner hangs up the phone, the dog loses interest in the game. This sort of dog would invariably rather be told off than be ignored.

For some dogs it is when the owner watches television that it feels it has to take control, and so it paces the room, and keeps crossing in front of the television in its efforts to get noticed. This dog usually recognizes certain theme tunes, and will start to demand attention as soon as it hears them. Sometimes the dog will bring the owner something to play with, and insist that the owner throws the object until it feels confident that it has the owner's undivided attention. It will then lose interest in the game, and the owner often finds it hard to get the dog to continue to play, even if the owner now wants to.

Quieting the attention-seeking barker

The most important part of this dog's treatment is for all of the owner's family to ignore completely all attempts by the dog to gain attention, unless the dog is asking to go to the toilet. Even then, some dogs will cotton on to this, and will then use asking to go to the toilet as a means of getting noticed, and will ask twenty times a day. Ignoring him means that if he tries to gain attention by nuzzling your arm to be stroked, barking, whining, bringing a toy to be played with, chasing his tail, trying to catch imaginary flies, or even if he simply sits staring at you, you should in no way respond. Even telling him to go away will be responding to what he has done, so you must not even do that. Sometimes he does something that makes him impossible to ignore, such as climbing into your lap. If he is a 12-stone Old English Mastiff and difficult to ignore at the best of times, stand up and walk away. If he starts barking and won't stop, use a can with pebbles in it to make him be quiet (information on how to do this is discussed in the chapter on predatory aggression). You can at times however, still do all of the things mentioned above, just never when he is telling you to do them. That way, you maintain control. Always do them when he is not telling you to, or if he has been demanding, wait for at least fifteen minutes, by which time he will have forgotten his own attempt, then you initiate the interaction. Once he realizes that demanding attention gets him exactly the opposite of what he wants, he will give up trying. Some owners find that when they try doing this, the dog refuses to respond. This emphasizes how important the dog sees gaining attention to be in regard to who is in control.

So if you have an anxious or attention-seeking, noisy dog:

1 Try to ascertain what the dog is trying to say.
2 Practise ignoring demands for attention, and teaching the dog to be more independent.
3 Find a way to make being isolated more rewarding.
4 Remove the dog from bedrooms and furniture.

If the dog is bored:

1 Pick up all toys and bones that are left lying around all of the time, and only leave down one or two of the less interesting ones.
2 Only put down the more interesting ones when you are going out, and pick them up again as soon as you return home.
3 You can also put down something more exciting such as a marrow-bone filled with soft cheese or fish paste, or a Kong toy filled in the same way.

17 Dogs That Are Sensitive to Certain Sounds

If you own a dog that is over-sensitive to sound, you know that it can be an irritating problem. But for some people, their dog's sensitivity goes far beyond a mere problem. Some dogs are so sensitive that they become difficult to live with, and place their owners under considerable pressure.

For the uninitiated, a dog that has this condition finds certain types of noises distressing. This distress can take several different visual forms. Some dogs will sit and whimper. Some dogs will run and hide. Some will even become aggressive towards the source of the noise. Noises that dogs are fearful of can range from vacuum cleaners to fireworks to thunder. Some are frightened of traffic noise, which makes them very difficult to exercise. Others are frightened of specific types of traffic, so they are fine with cars, but are terrified of buses or lorries. Some are aggressive towards trains, and will chase them barking and growling. You often find dogs that react to a whole range of sounds of a particular type. For example, some dogs will hate any kind of bang such as gunfire. Others will hate wailing noises like sirens.

For years owners have had to accept these situations. They learn to avoid busy roads to stop the dog being frightened by the traffic, or they tranquillize the dog to stop it reacting to the thunder and lightning. However, it is now accepted that dogs can be desensitized to these sounds, so that they no longer react in a fearful manner.

Case History – Time to put theory to test, on my own dog

My own dogs had always been fine about any type of noise. They were not bothered by the sound of traffic, thunder, fireworks or any of the other noises with which many dogs have difficulty coping. They had always been exposed to different kinds of noises to avoid this problem manifesting itself.

However, in October 1987, the south of England was hit by a terrible storm. Trees hundreds of years old were torn from the ground as though they were twigs. Roofs were pulled from buildings, indeed many buildings themselves were completely destroyed. Cars were overturned as though they weighed nothing.

I awoke during this hurricane to find my older dog, Caesar, in a very stressed state. He was panting heavily, and pacing the room. The storm had obviously disturbed him greatly. All night he wouldn't settle, until the wind and rain finally died out in the early hours.

That night was the beginning of Caesar developing an aversion to loud noises. Like most dogs that end up fearing a variety of sounds, he was originally only afraid of one particular noise: thunder. But as is so often the case, the fear then spreads to other, similar sounds. The dog that was once only afraid of thunder will eventually be afraid of thunder, cars backfiring, fireworks and anything else that bangs. And this was the case with Caesar. He went from only being afraid of thunder to being frightened of any sudden bang. He would sense a storm coming half an hour before the first clap of thunder or drop of rain. Fortunately for me, his hearing was already deteriorating, so the problem didn't last long.

For some owners however, this behaviour can be very difficult to live with.

Case History – Certainly not this dog's favourite airline!

The owner of this dog phoned me as she was 'absolutely desperate, and prepared to try anything.' Her dog, a 4-year-old crossbreed, disliked aeroplanes. In fact, he disliked them to such a degree that as soon as he heard one, he would fly into a tantrum of barking, growling and dashing about. If he was in the garden he would run at the fence as the plane went over, roaring his head off as though he believed that he was chasing the plane away himself. If he was inside he would dash to the door barking frantically to be let out so that he could see it off. What made matters worse was that the owner lived in a Concorde flight path, and when that particular plane went over, the dog would nearly have a heart attack, such was his excitement.

Needless to say, with as many as twenty planes a day going directly over the owner's house, the situation had become intolerable. Apart from the owner's shattered nerves, the neighbours had started to complain, and she had received an anonymous letter threatening her with the local authority noise pollution department if she didn't 'shut that dog up!'

The reason that the dog developed this behaviour is unclear. The owner could not pin-point any particular time that he first began to show an aggressive response to aircraft. The cure involved a program of training an incompatible behaviour, with a dash of desensitization, coupled with some habituation. Desensitization means changing the dog's attitude to a stimulus by teaching him to associate that stimulus with something rewarding. Habituation involves simply exposing the dog to the stimulus at such a frequent degree that he no longer reacts to it.

So firstly, we taught the dog an incompatible behaviour, which involved teaching him to lie down immediately on command. This would make it impossible for him to run after planes barking. The next stage was to associate the sound of planes with his favourite thing in the world: food. The owner recorded the sound of various planes on to a tape. She would switch on the tape and immediately give the dog the 'DOWN' command. Once he dropped, the owner would throw him several treats while the tape was still running. The owner would then keep the dog in the 'down' until the sound of the plane died away. When the next plane on the tape came on, the process would be repeated. Once the dog had begun to make the connection between hearing a plane and lying down for food, we then started to leave the tape running for several minutes continually after each plane, as a form of habituation. This would cause him to begin to lose interest in the sound of the planes. We then started to alter the type of reward, so that instead of always getting food, we now only gave food occasionally, and usually gave either verbal or physical praise instead. These two things would have the effect of making the sound of planes less significant to the dog. The next thing to do was to practise the same thing outdoors, which we did in the owner's back garden. Once we had got him to drop on command and expect food in the garden, we then taught him to do the same thing in the park. This was actually harder for the owner than it was for the dog, as she had to overcome her embarrassment at playing a tape recording of aeroplanes in a public place for the benefit of her dog. But it comes down to how great you consider a problem to be, and how determined you are to put that problem right. Remember, if you are too embarrassed to train your dog, the ones likely to suffer most will be you, your family and your dog. As a result of all her hard work, the owner found that the dog would still look up at the sound of a plane overhead, but she found that he gradually lost interest in these too after a while.

So if you have a dog that is sound over-sensitive, try to:

1   Teach the dog a behaviour or position that makes it difficult or impossible for the dog to do what you do not want it to (incompatible behaviour).
2   Record the sound and play it to the dog at times when the dog is relaxed or excited and happy. Play the tape in many different environments, so that the dog is not stressed about that sound anywhere that it hears it (de-sensitization).
3   Gradually expose the dog to the sound more and more, until he is so used to it it becomes boring (habituation).

Useful Addresses

The Animal Health Trust
P.O. Box 5, Newmarket, Suffolk CB8 7DW. Tel: (01638)
661111

Battersea Dogs Home
4, Battersea Park Road, London, SW8 4AA. Tel: 020 7622
3626

The Blue Cross Animal Welfare Society
Field Centre, Shilton Road, Burford, Oxon OX8 4PF. Tel:
(01993) 822651

The Celia Hammond Animal Trust
233, Lewisham Way, London SE4 1UY. Tel: 020 8691 2100

Dog Aid
25, Speechley Drive, Rugeley, Staffordshire, WS15 2PT. Tel:
(01889) 579103

Guide Dogs For The Blind
Alexandra House, 9, Park Street, Windsor, Berkshire SL4
1JR. Tel: (01739) 835555

Hearing Dogs For The Deaf
London Road, Lewknor, Oxford, OX9 5RY. Tel: (01844) 353898

The Kennel Club
1, Clarges Street, London W1Y 8AB. Tel: 020 7493 6651

Last Chance Animal Rescue
Stick Hill, Edenbridge, Kent TN8 5NH. Tel: (01732) 865530

The National Canine Defence League (N.C.D.L.)
17, Wakley Street, London EC1V 7RQ. Tel: 020 7837 0006

The People's Dispensary For Sick Animals (P.D.S.A.)
Regional Head Office, Hurst Road, South Croydon, CRO 1JT. Tel: 020 8686 3872

The Royal College Of Veterinary Surgeons
32, Belgrave Square, London, SW1X 8QP. Tel: 020 7235 4971

The Royal Society For The Prevention Of Cruelty To Animals (R.S.P.C.A.)
National Headquarters, Causeway, Horsham, West Sussex RH12 1HG. Tel: (01403) 264181

The UK Registry of Canine Behaviourists
Registered Office: Dunsmore Kennels, London Road (A45), Stretton-on-Dunsmore, Warwickshire, CV23 9HX. Tel: (01203) 542566

Wood Green Animal Shelter
Kings Bush Farm, London Road, Godmanchester, Huntingdon, Cambridgeshire PE18 8LJ. Tel: (01480) 830014

Recommended Reading

Coren, Stanley, *The Intelligence of Dogs* (Bantam, New York, 1995)

Dodman, Nicholas, *The Dog Who Loved Too Much* (Bantam, New York, 1996)

Dunbar, Ian, *Dog Behaviour – Why Dogs Do What They Do* (TFH Publications, New Jersey, 1979)

Fogle, Dr Bruce, *The Encyclopaedia of the Dog* (Dorling Kindersley, 1996)

Hunter, Roy, *Fun and Games with Dogs* (Howln Moon Press, Maine, 1993)

O'Farrell, Valerie, *Manual of Canine Behaviour* (British Small Animal Veterinary Association, 1986)

Rogerson, John, *In Tune with Your Dog* (Popular Dogs Publishing, 1997)

——, *Training Your Dog* (Popular Dogs Publishing, 1992)

Ryan, Terry, *The Toolbox for Remodelling Your Problem Dog* (Howell Book House, New York, 1998)

Sandys-Winsch, Godfrey, *The Dog Law Handbook* (Shaw & Sons, 1993)

Taylor, David, *The Ultimate Dog Book* (Dorling Kindersley, 1996)

Volhard, Wendy, & Kerry Brown DVM, *The Holistic Guide to a Healthy Dog* (Howell Book House, New York, 1995)

Index

Activity toy, 203
Afgan Hound, 36
Aggression, 138–86
  Chase/predatory, 27, 175, 178
  Dominant, 30, 33–4, 42, 64–6, 144–56
  Fear-based, 138–44
  Food, 31–2, 161–5
  Pack order, 165–74
  Territorial, 29, 157–61
Alaskan Malamute, 14, 34
American Pit Bull Terrier, 88
Animals Act (1971), 128
Attention-seeking, 179, 186, 190, 193–4, 197, 201, 204, 206–8
Audio tape, 50

Barking, 158, 160, 193, 201–8, 209
Basenji, 35
Basset, 35
Battersea Dogs Home, 88
Beagle, 35
Bearded Collie, 169
Biting, 147–8
Blue Cross, 67

Border Collie, 14, 26, 77, 78, 107, 160, 175, 185
Border Terrier, 146–7
Boxer, 28, 62
Breed Characteristics, 26–39
Breeders, 21, 23, 29, 30, 33, 36, 39, 169
Breeding of Dogs Act (1973), 131

Cairn Terrier, 33
Canis
  Aureus, 14
  Lupus, 14
  Simensis, 14
Castration, 81, 146, 174 (see chapter 6)
Cats, 25, 35, 38, 175, 178, 201
Cavalier King Charles Spaniel, 32, 180
Check chain, 110, 114–17, 161, 177
Chihuahua, 72
Children, 20, 22, 25, 27–8, 30, 34, 38, 40–51, 54, 71, 76, 83, 127, 146, 147, 175
Chow Chow, 34
Clipping, 24

Cocker Spaniel, 32, 163
Communication, 90–5
Crossbreeds, 20, 24, 91, 162, 172, 211

Dalmation, 29
Dangerous Dogs Act (1991), 129
Desensitization, 141, 212
Destruction, 27, 56, 77, 96, 189, 189–96, 202, 203
Dobermann Pinscher, 29–30
Dogs Act (1871), 129
Dried foods, 73

English Bull Terrier, 34, 152, 154, 182, 207
Exercise, 27, 29, 56, 67, 72, 74–7, 80, 127, 154

Feeding, 56, 62, 72–6, 131–2, 141, 162–3
Fighting, 33, 142, 144, 168–9
Fireworks, 209, 210
Fleas, 69–70
Flank-sucking, 30
Fouling indoors, 33, 96, 105, 165

German Shepherd Dog, 14, 28–9, 107–8, 114, 126, 142, 144, 157, 167, 172
Golden Retriever, 31, 175
Great Dane, 14, 41, 72, 76, 138, 141, 179, 187, 188
Greyhound, 35, 88
Grooming, 24–5, 36, 68, 136

Guard dogs, 19, 30, 129, 130
Guard Dogs Act (1975), 129
Gundogs, 31–2, 36, 163

Habituation, 212
Head collar, 115
Health, 67–78, 127
Heelwork, 113–17, 114
Hip dysplasia, 29
Hounds, 35
House training, see fouling indoors
Husky, 13, 14
Hygiene, 68

Identification, 87–9
Idiopathic aggression, 152–5
Insurance, 24, 68
Irish Setter, 32

Jack Russell, 33, 76, 97, 104
Japanese Tosa, 88

Kennel Club, The, 21, 38, 214
Kennels, 30, 59
Kong toy, 203, 208

Labrador Retriever, 31, 36, 62, 99, 110, 140, 161, 190
Lhasa Apso, 76
Lick lesions, 30
Livestock, 130–1

Marrow bone, 200, 202
Mastiff, 30, 78, 207
Mating, 23, 84, 128
Mental stimulation, 27

Microchipping, 88

Neutering, 24, 58, 74, 79–86, 129, 156, 180
Newfoundland, 31

Obedience training, 102–29
Oil of clove, 176
Old English Sheepdog, 14, 19, 30
Older dogs, 25–6, 53, 143, 172

Papillon, 125
Parasites, 69
PDSA, 67
Pedigree, 20, 23, 24, 38, 131
Pekingese, 76
Pet shops, 23, 37, 38, 70, 130, 200
Poodle, 24, 36
Poop scoops, 128
Predatory aggression, 25, 27, 160, 175, 207
Protection of Livestock Act (1953), 130
Puppy, 19–26, 31, 36–9, 68, 77, 83, 103–6, 118, 119, 131, 143, 147–9, 183–5, 198–200
Pyometra, 79

Rage syndrome, 32
Raw meat, 73
Rescue centres, 21, 26, 30, 39, 131

Rottweiler, 30, 52, 99, 138, 145
Rough Collie, 28, 159
Roundworms, 71–2
RSPCA, 67, 88

Saint Bernard, 76
Samoyed, 14, 34
Scent marking, 79, 105, 127
Schizophrenia, 37
Schnauzer, 24, 159
Scottish Terrier, 33
Shih Tzu, 64, 166
Socializing, 22, 25, 122
Sound deterrent, 56, 161, 177
Sound sensitivity, 209–13
Spaying, see chapter 6
Springer Spaniel, 149
Squirrels, 38, 175, 178, 201
Staffordshire Bull Terrier, 33–4, 183
Stay on command, 120–2
Straying, 80, 126–8
Stripping, 24

Tapeworms, 71
Terriers, 33, 36, 76, 168
Ticks, 70
Tinned foods, 73
Testicular tumours, 80
Toxocara canis, 71
Toy dogs, 32
Treats, 43, 47–9, 116, 139, 140–1, 150, 157, 161, 167, 171, 174, 176, 200, 212

Utility dogs, 36–9

Vaccinations, 24, 68–9, 118,
143, 184

Weight
gain, 74–5
loss, 75–6
Weimaraner, 14, 32, 87
West Highland White Terrier,
24, 33, 53, 54
Whistle, 47
Wolf, 13–15, 34
Working dogs, 26–30, 36
Worms, 71–2
Worrying livestock, 130

Yorkshire Terrier, 125